# Seventh-day Adventism

# Seventh-day Adventism

*by*

ANTHONY A. HOEKEMA

WILLIAM B. EERDMANS PUBLISHING COMPANY
Grand Rapids, Michigan

The material in this book is an updating of
material originally appearing in *The Four
Major Cults*, Fourth Printing, August 1972.

# Contents

5

# Preface

The discussion of Seventh-day Adventism found in this book is organized as follows: First, a brief history of the movement is given, including the main facts about the life of Ellen G. White, and followed by the most recent statistics about the church: membership figures, publishing houses, schools, hospitals, and the like. Next the question of the final source of authority appealed to by Seventh-day Adventists is taken up. Then the doctrines taught by the Seventh-day Adventist Church are expounded in the order of the customary divisions of Christian theology: God, man, Christ, salvation, the church, the last things. Two appendixes are added, which offer Scriptural and historical material in refutation of certain Adventist teachings: Appendix A, dealing with the investigative judgment and the scapegoat doctrine, and Appendix B, dealing with the Sabbath question.

In setting forth the doctrinal teachings of the Seventh-day Adventist Church, I have used primary sources exclusively (the writings of Ellen G. White and doctrinal works by Adventist leaders, particularly a recent official statement of Seventh-day Adventist teachings entitled *Questions on Doctrine*). Whenever there was uncertainty about what was being taught on a particular doctrinal point, information was obtained directly from Seventh-day Adventist leaders. References to the source materials used are given in the footnotes. A bibliography lists Mrs. White's major writings, histories of Seventh-day Adventism, Seventh-day Adventist publications, and a number of general works. All Scripture quotations not otherwise identified are from the American Standard Version.

Readers of this book are referred to the author's *Four Major Cults* (Eerdmans, 1963) for further material. One will find in the last-

7

named volume an appendix, not found in the present work, which deals critically with teachings common to both Seventh-day Adventists and Jehovah's Witnesses on "soul-extinction" in the intermediate state and on the final annihilation of the wicked. Besides setting forth the doctrinal teachings of Christian Science, Jehovah's Witnesses, and Mormonism, *The Four Major Cults* also includes chapters on the challenge of the cults, the distinctive traits of the cult, and the approach to the cultist.

May the Lord use this book for the advancement of His kingdom and for the glory of His name.

Anthony A. Hoekema

*Grand Rapids, Michigan*
*July, 1972*

# I. History

## WILLIAM MILLER

THOUGH WILLIAM MILLER (1782-1849) NEVER JOINED THE SEVenth-day Adventist movement, the history of Seventh-day Adventism has its roots in Miller's prophecies. Miller was born in Pittsfield, Massachusetts, in 1782. While he was still young, his family moved to Low Hampton, New York, close to the Vermont border. Though he had been reared in a Christian home, Miller became a complete skeptic, rejecting the Bible as divine revelation. After a term in the army he turned to farming, and became a respected member of the Low Hampton community. In 1816 he was converted from his skepticism. During the next two years he studied the Bible intensively with the aid of Cruden's Concordance, but without the help of commentaries. In 1818 he wrote down the conclusions to which he had arrived, which ended with this statement: "I was thus brought, in 1818, at the close of my two-year study of the Scriptures, to the solemn conclusion, that in about twenty-five years from that time [1818] all the affairs of our present state would be wound up."[1] In other words, Miller concluded from his Bible study that the world would come to an end in 1843.

Hesitant about publicizing so startling a conclusion, he undertook four more years of Bible study, which confirmed his previous judgment. In 1831, at the request of a friend, he publicly stated his views. This led to frequent requests to speak, so that in 1834 he became a full-time Baptist preacher. As can be understood,

[1] Leroy Edwin Froom, *The Prophetic Faith of our Fathers* (Washington: Review and Herald, 1954), IV, 463.

he preached chiefly on prophecy and the Second Coming of Christ. As can also be understood, he soon had quite a following.

Involved in the "winding up" of the affairs of the world was, of course, the expected return from heaven of the Lord Jesus Christ. Miller did not at first set an exact date for Christ's return, but affirmed that this event would occur "about 1843." Later, however, he specified that this return would take place some time during the Jewish year running from March 21, 1843 to March 21, 1844.[2]

How did Miller arrive at this date? In Daniel 9:24-27 he found the prophecy of the "seventy weeks" which are there predicted as extending from the commandment to rebuild Jerusalem (v. 25) to the time when the anointed one shall be cut off (v. 26). Miller took the starting point for these seventy weeks to be the decree of Artaxerxes spoken of in Ezra 7:11-26 which permitted Ezra to go back to Jerusalem, this decree being dated in his Bible (according to the Ussher chronology) as having been issued in 457 B.C. He assumed that in prophetic writings of this sort a day stood for a year.[3] On this basis seventy weeks, which would be equivalent to 490 days, would represent 490 years. And 490 years after 457 B.C brings us to A.D. 33, the year when, according to Ussher, Christ was crucified.

In Daniel 8:14 there is a reference to 2300 evenings and mornings which must elapse before the sanctuary shall be cleansed. Miller assumed that the cleansing of the sanctuary alluded to in this prophecy meant Christ's return to earth. In agreement with the principle stated in the preceding paragraph, he took the 2300 evenings and mornings as standing for 2300 years. He also assumed that the 2300 years started at the same time as the 70 weeks. And 2300 years after 457 B.C. brings us to A.D. 1843, the year when, according to Miller, Christ would return.[4]

It should be noted at this time that this calculation rests on five unproved assumptions: (1) that a day in prophetic writings always represents a year; (2) that the 70 weeks and the 2300

---

[2] Francis D. Nichol, *The Midnight Cry* (Washington: Review and Herald, 1945), p. 169.

[3] Froom, *op. cit.,* IV, 473.

[4] *Ibid.* Seventh-day Adventists still follow Miller's method of calculation — see *Seventh-day Adventists Answer Questions on Doctrine* (Washington: Review and Herald, 1957), pp. 268-95. The only difference is, as we shall see, that they have a different interpretation of the cleansing of the sanctuary than Miller did.

days began at the same time; (3) that this starting date was 457 B.C.;[5] (4) that in figuring the *terminus ad quem* we need make no allowance for the fact that March 21, 0 B.C., would actually be March 21, A.D. 1, thus throwing the calculation off by one year; and (5) that the cleansing of the sanctuary spoken of in Daniel 8:14 stands for Christ's return to earth.[6]

When the designated year arrived, however, the Lord did not return, and there was intense disappointment in the ranks of the so-called "Millerites." Miller, though dumbfounded at the failure of his calculations, was still sure that he had been right. He said,

> Were I to live my life over again, with the same evidence that I then had, to be honest with God and man, I should have to do as I have done. . . . I confess my error, and acknowledge my disappointment; yet I still believe that the day of the Lord is near, even at the door; and I exhort you, my brethren, to be watchful, and not let that day come upon you unawares.[7]

In August of 1844, however, Samuel S. Snow, one of the Millerite leaders, launched the so-called "seventh-month movement." He had become convinced that the 2300 days of Daniel 8:14 were to end not in the spring of 1844, as Miller had supposed, but in the fall of that year. Specifically, he predicted that Christ would return on October 22, 1844, which would be our calendar equivalent of the Jewish Day of Atonement for that year.[8] The "seventh-month movement" — so called because Tishri, the month in which the Day of Atonement fell, was the seventh month of the Jewish

---

[5] If we were inclined to engage in this type of calculation (which most of us probably are not), it should be noted that the decree of Artaxerxes spoken of in Ezra 7 had nothing to do with the rebuilding of Jerusalem. Yet Daniel spoke of the "commandment" (literally, "word," *dabhar*) to restore and to build Jerusalem. It would seem that Artaxerxes' decision to permit Nehemiah to go back to the city of his fathers' sepulchres, so that he might rebuild it (Neh. 2:5-8), would be much more to the point. But this happened thirteen years after 457 B.C., in 444 B.C. Seventh-day Adventists, however, still defend Miller's choice of 457 B.C.

[6] It is interesting to note that the word translated "cleansed" in the King James Version of Dan. 8:14 is actually the Niphal form of the Hebrew verb *tsadaq*, which means to be right or righteous. Hence the RSV renders the last part of the verse, "then the sanctuary shall be restored to its rightful state"; and the Berkeley version has "then the rights of the sanctuary shall be restored." Many commentators accordingly understand the passage as a prediction of the recovery of the Jerusalem temple from Antiochus Epiphanes by Judas Maccabeus in 165 B.C.

[7] Sylvester Bliss, *Memoirs of William Miller*, p. 256; quoted in Nichol, *The Midnight Cry*, p. 171.

[8] Froom, *op. cit.*, IV, 799-800.

ecclesiastical year — rapidly gained momentum; before long virtually all the followers of Miller had accepted this re-interpretation
of the 2300-day prophecy, including, finally, even Miller himself.[9]
As October 22 approached, excitement mounted. Groups of
Millerites gathered in their homes and in their meeting-places,
expecting the Lord to return some time that day. As October 22
ended, however, and Christ did not return, the disappointment of
the Millerites was overwhelming. In fact, this day is usually referred to in their history as the day of "The Great Disappointment."[10] Many now gave up the "Advent" faith; but others still
clung to it.

### HIRAM EDSON

As we continue our discussion of the history of Seventh-day
Adventism, we must further take note of three individuals who
played key roles in the development of this movement. The first
of these is Hiram Edson of Port Gibson, New York (not far from
Rochester). A group of "Millerite" believers met at Edson's
house, about a mile south of Port Gibson, on October 22, 1844, to
wait for Christ's return. Among those closely associated with
Edson at that time were a physician, Dr. Franklin B. Hahn, and a
student in his early twenties, O. R. L. Crosier. On the following
morning most of the believers, greatly disappointed, returned to
their homes. With those who remained, Edson went to his barn
to pray. They prayed until they felt assured that light would be
given them and that their disappointment would be explained.[11]

After breakfast Edson decided to go out to comfort the other
Adventists with the assurance they had received through prayer.
Edson and a companion (who is surmised by most Adventist
writers to have been Crosier) walked across the corn field adjoin-
ing the farm on their way to their first destination. At this point
I quote from a manuscript written by Edson himself:

> We started, and while passing through a large field I was
> stopped about midway of the field. Heaven seemed open to my
> view, and I saw distinctly and clearly that instead of our
> High Priest coming out of the Most Holy of the heavenly

[9] *Ibid.*, pp. 818-20.
[10] Walter R. Martin, *The Truth About Seventh-day Adventism* (Grand
Rapids: Zondervan, 1960), p. 29.
[11] Arthur W. Spalding, on pp. 91-105 of his *Captains of the Host*
(Washington: Review and Herald, 1949), gives a vivid account of this
entire episode and of the events connected with it.

sanctuary to come to this earth on the tenth day of the seventh month, at the end of the 2300 days, He for the first time entered on that day the second apartment of that sanctuary; and that He had a work to perform in the most holy before coming to this earth.[12]

Edson told his companion about his vision, which appeared to both of them to be the Lord's answer to their prayer of that morning. In the light of this vision, Edson now realized that there was a heavenly sanctuary corresponding to the Old Testament earthly sanctuary which had been patterned after it, and that there were two phases in Christ's heavenly ministry, just as there had been two phases in the sanctuary ministry of Old Testament priests. In other words, the light now dawned upon him that, instead of Christ's having come out of the holy of holies of the heavenly sanctuary to this earth at the end of the 2300 days, he had simply for the first time passed from the holy place of the heavenly sanctuary into the heavenly holy of holies. So Miller had not been wrong in his calculations, but simply in thinking that the sanctuary which was to be cleansed at the end of the 2300-day period was a sanctuary on earth — or, perhaps, the earth itself.

During the next several months Edson, Hahn, and Crosier set themselves to earnest Bible study, particularly with regard to the sanctuary ministry as described both in the Old Testament and in the book of Hebrews. Crosier wrote up his conclusions on the subject in an article which appeared in the Cincinnati *Day-Star,* an Adventist publication, under date of February 7, 1846. Froom, in his *Prophetic Faith of our Fathers,* gives a digest of this article.[13] Crosier explained that we must see in the work of Christ a fulfillment of the work of the Old Testament priests. In the daily work of these priests, when they presented the daily offerings to God and brought the blood of these offerings into the holy place, sprinkling it before the veil or applying it to the horns of the altar of incense, they were only transferring iniquity from the people to the sanctuary (p. 1232).[14] On the Great Day of Atone-

---

[12] From a fragment of a manuscript on his life and experiences, by Hiram Edson; quoted by Nichol, *The Midnight Cry,* p. 458.

[13] Vol. IV, pp. 1228-34. He also gives his own understanding of the views of Crosier and Edson, expanding somewhat on the Crosier article, on pp. 896-900.

[14] Froom gives his own interpretation of the meaning of these actions when he says, "Thus in symbol the sins of the people were borne into the sanctuary, to the entrance of the Most Holy, thus 'polluting' the sanctuary" (pp. 896-97).

ment, however, the sanctuary was cleansed. This happened, so
Crosier continued, when the high priest entered the holy of holies
and sprinkled the blood of the slain goat upon the mercy seat
(p. 1232).[15] After the sanctuary had been cleansed, the sins of
the people were then put on the head of the scapegoat which was
sent away into the wilderness (p. 1232). There were thus two
phases in the ministry of the Old Testament priests: the first
(the daily ministry, which had to do with the holy place) led to
the forgiveness of sins; the second, however (the yearly ministry,
which had to do with the holy of holies), led to the blotting out
of sins (p. 1232).[16]

These two phases of priestly ministry, Crosier continued, are
also to be seen in the work of Christ. Throughout the centuries
of the Christian era Christ had been doing a work comparable to
the daily ministry of the priests, which work resulted in the forgiveness of sin but not in the blotting out of sin (p. 1233). The
process of blotting out sin began on October 22, 1844, when Christ
entered the holy of holies of the heavenly sanctuary, an action
which was comparable to the work of the high priest on the Day
of Atonement. However, since the cleansing of the sanctuary
was not complete until the sins of the people had been laid on the
scapegoat — who, Crosier explained, typified not Christ but
Satan — the last act of Christ's priestly ministry will be to take
the sins from the heavenly sanctuary and to place them on Satan
(pp. 1233-34). Only after this has happened will Christ return
(p. 1234).[17]

Later in Adventist history the concept of Christ's having entered
the heavenly holy of holies was to be expanded into the so-called
"investigative judgment" doctrine, which we shall examine later.

[15] The reader will note at this point a most peculiar inconsistency.
Whereas the application of sacrificial blood to the altar of incense in the
holy place is said to *pollute* the sanctuary (since the sins of believers
are thus brought into the sanctuary), the application of sacrificial blood
to the mercy seat in the holy of holies is said to *cleanse* the sanctuary.
Why should the same ritual procedure pollute in the one case and cleanse
in the other?

[16] This distinction between forgiveness and blotting out should be
carefully noted; it plays an important part in subsequent Seventh-day
Adventist theology.

[17] Froom adds that the Crosier article represented the views, not only
of Crosier himself, but also of Edson and Hahn. He further states that
the article was endorsed by such prominent Adventist leaders as Joseph
Bates and Ellen G. White; it may thus be taken as representative of
Adventist thought at this time.

Already at this time, however, Adventists had found a solution to the "Great Disappointment," and had laid the groundwork for their later teachings on Christ's present ministry in the heavenly sanctuary.[18]

## JOSEPH BATES

A second person prominent in the early history of Seventh-day Adventism was Joseph Bates. This man, during twenty-one years at sea, had advanced from cabin boy to captain and ship owner. He had been converted to Christianity on board ship. After retirement he took up residence in Fair Haven, Massachusetts, where he joined the Christian Connection Church. From 1839 onward Bates was in the forefront of the Advent movement. Through the reading of an article on the Sabbath by Thomas M. Preble in the Portland (Maine) *Hope of Israel* of February 28, 1845, Bates became convinced that the seventh day was the proper Sabbath for Christians to observe.[19]

Previous to this time a group of Adventists in Washington, New Hampshire, had been influenced by some Seventh-day Baptists to embrace the seventh day as the Sabbath. This all began through the influence of a woman — Mrs. Rachel Oakes. She, having become a Seventh-day Baptist, was attending an Adventist communion service in Washington one Sunday in the winter of 1843. After the preacher, Frederick Wheeler, had called upon all his hearers to "obey God and keep His commandments in all things," Mrs. Oakes almost arose to object. Afterwards she told the preacher that she had wanted to ask him to put the cloth back over the communion table until he was willing to keep *all* the commandments of God, *including the fourth*. Knowing that Mrs. Oakes was a Seventh-day Baptist, Wheeler promised her that he would do some serious thinking and earnest studying on the Sabbath question. In March of 1844 he arrived at the conclusion that the seventh day was the proper Sabbath, and began to observe it. Shortly afterwards the leaders of the Adventist group in Washington accepted this view, and began to observe the seventh day.

[18] It should be noted at this time that William Miller, who died in 1849, never accepted Crosier's teachings about Christ's sanctuary ministry (Froom, *op. cit.*, IV, 828-9). It is also significant to note that Crosier himself later repudiated his earlier teachings on the sanctuary (*ibid.*, p 892, n. 18).

[19] Froom, *op. cit.*, IV, 953-55.

The Washington, New Hampshire, Adventists were thus the first Adventists to observe the seventh day.[20]

After Joseph Bates had arrived at his conclusions about the Sabbath Day, he heard about what had happened at Washington, New Hampshire, and visited the leaders there, including Frederick Wheeler. This visit strengthened Bates's convictions about the Sabbath Day.[21]

Early in 1846 Bates wrote a forty-eight-page tract entitled *The Seventh-day Sabbath, a Perpetual Sign*. In it he argued that the seventh-day Sabbath had been prefigured in creation, ordained in Eden, and confirmed at Mount Sinai. In 1847 he wrote a second edition of this tract, in which he discussed the messages of the three angels of Revelation 14:6-12. The third angel mentioned in this passage threatens dire punishments upon those who worship the beast and his image, and who receive his mark on their foreheads (v. 9). Identifying the beast with the Papacy, and arguing that it was the Papacy which had changed the Sabbath from the seventh day to the first, Bates concluded that those who still kept the first day as the Sabbath were worshiping the papal beast and would thus receive his mark. The obedience to God's commandments required by the third angel, Bates continued, was to consist particularly in the observance of the seventh day.[22]

In January, 1849, Bates issued a second tract, entitled *A Seal of the Living God*. Noting that, according to Revelation 7, the servants of God were sealed on their foreheads, Bates concluded that the seventh-day Sabbath was the seal of God here spoken of. From the fact that the number of the sealed spoken of in this chapter is 144,000, Bates drew the conclusion that the "remnant" who keep the commandments of God — in other words, the faithful Adventists — would number only 144,000.[23]

Thus there was added to the Adventist movement an emphasis on the keeping of the seventh day as the Sabbath. Though at first Bates's argument on the Sabbath did not appeal to Ellen Harmon and James White (who were to become prominent Adventist leaders), later they also accepted this position.[24] It was therefore now

---

[20] *Ibid.*, pp. 944-47.
[21] *Ibid.*, pp. 947-48.
[22] *Ibid.*, pp. 956-58.
[23] *Ibid.*, p. 958. Walter Martin indicates, however, that this early restriction of the remnant to 144,000 has been repudiated by the Seventh-day Adventist denomination (*The Truth About Seventh-day Adventism*, p. 34, n. 12).
[24] Froom, *op. cit.*, p. 959.

taught by Adventists that the keeping of the seventh day was the "seal of God," the characteristic mark of all of God's true children. The observance of the first day of the week as the Lord's Day, however, was interpreted as an action which would make one liable to receive the "mark of the beast," and to drink the cup of God's anger.

### ELLEN G. WHITE

The third important figure who played a leading role in the history of Seventh-day Adventism was Ellen G. White (1827-1915). Ellen Gould Harmon was born in 1827 in Gorham, Maine, some ten miles north of Portland. While Ellen was still a child, her family moved to Portland. Here they were members of the Chestnut Street Methodist Church. When Ellen was nine years old, while going home from school, she was struck in the face by a stone thrown by an older girl. She was unconscious for three weeks; her nose was broken and her face was disfigured. ". . . The shock to her nervous system and the illness which followed, with succeeding complications, continued for years to make her an invalid and to present a constant threat to her life."[25]

In 1840 and in 1842 William Miller lectured in Portland on the Second Advent. After having attended these lectures, the Harmon family accepted Miller's teachings, and were, as a result, disfellowshiped from the Methodist church. It was after the Great Disappointment of 1844 that Ellen had her first vision: in December of that year, while visiting with some other Adventist women at the home of a friend, and while kneeling in prayer, she saw in a vision the Advent believers traveling along a lighted pathway until they reached the shining City of God. Jesus was the guide and leader of this group, which grew to become a great company.[26] Shortly after this, a second vision revealed that, though she was bound to encounter disbelief and calumny, she must now tell others what God had shown her.[27] She now began a life of public witnessing, counseling, teaching, and writing. On August 30, 1846, she married James White, a young Adventist preacher who had been active in the Millerite movement. From this union four sons were born.[28]

[25] Spalding, *op. cit.,* p. 62.
[26] Froom, *op. cit.,* IV, 979, 981-82.
[27] *Ibid.,* p. 980.
[28] Francis D. Nichol, *Ellen G. White and her Critics* (Washington: Review and Herald, 1951), p. 36.

Soon there was a sizable group of Advent believers around Portland, Maine, who began to recognize that Mrs. White was being uniquely guided by the Holy Spirit — that, in fact, she was a true prophetess, whose visions and words were to be followed. Others in the Advent movement came to accept Mrs. White's leadership.

Mrs. White's husband stated that during the earlier part of her ministry she had from one hundred to two hundred "open visions" in twenty-three years. These "open visions," however, decreased as the years passed, later guidance coming to her through messages in her waking hours or through dreams. Almost every aspect of the belief and activity of the Seventh-day Adventists was encouraged or inspired by a vision or word from Mrs. White. Thus, in February of 1845, she had a vision of Jesus entering into the holy of holies of the heavenly sanctuary, confirming Hiram Edson's vision received in October of the preceding year.[29] On April 7, 1847, she had a vision in which she was taken first into the holy place, and then into the holy of holies of the heavenly sanctuary. There she saw the ark and the Ten Commandments in the ark, with a halo of glory around the Sabbath commandment.[30] This vision, therefore, confirmed Joseph Bates's teachings about the seventh day. In her voluminous writings Mrs. White commented on such diversified subjects as salvation in all its phases, sacred history, Christian doctrine, the home and society, health, education, temperance, evangelism, finance, world missions, the organization of the church, and the inspiration of the Bible.[31]

The attitude of present-day Seventh-day Adventists toward Mrs. White is well expressed in the following statement, in which Francis Nichol describes the second of two distinguishing marks which set the Advent movement apart: "The belief that God gave to this movement, in harmony with the forecast of prophecy, a manifestation of the prophetic gift in the person and writings of Mrs. E. G. White."[32] Still more official is the following statement, taken from Article 19 of the "Fundamental Beliefs of Seventh-day Adventists":

> That the gift of the Spirit of prophecy is one of the identifying marks of the remnant church. . . . They [Seventh-day Adventists]

[29] *Ibid.,* p. 178.
[30] *Ibid.,* p. 189, n. 2.
[31] Froom, *op. cit.,* IV, 985-86.
[32] *Ellen G. White and her Critics,* p. 22.

recognize that this gift was manifested in the life and ministry of Ellen G. White.[33]

In a later section of this chapter we shall examine this claim in order to see what light it sheds on the question of the source of authority for Seventh-day Adventism.

### THE SEVENTH-DAY ADVENTIST CHURCH

We have just reviewed the teachings of three Millerite Adventist groups: the group headed by Hiram Edson in western New York State, which emphasized the doctrine of the heavenly sanctuary; the group in Washington, New Hampshire, which, along with Joseph Bates, advocated the observance of the seventh day; and the group around Portland, Maine, which held that Ellen G. White was a true prophetess, whose visions and words were to be followed by the Adventists. These three groups fused to form the Seventh-day Adventist denomination.[34] It might be added that the three teachings developed by these groups (the Sabbath, the sanctuary, and the spirit of prophecy) formed the basis for the emergence of the new theological system known as Seventh-day Adventism,[35] and continue to be among the most distinctive doctrines of that movement.

Through the missionary efforts of Joseph Bates, Adventist groups were started in Jackson, Michigan, and in Battle Creek, Michigan; soon the latter town became the location for the first headquarters of the movement. In 1860 the name *Seventh-day Adventist* was adopted as the official name of the denomination; in May of 1863 the first General Conference, with representatives from all the state conferences except Vermont, was held in Battle Creek. We recognize the year 1863, therefore, as the date of the official organization of the Seventh-day Adventist denomination.[36] In 1903 both General Conference Headquarters and the Review and Herald Publishing Association were moved to Takoma Park, a suburb of Washington, D. C.[37]

[33] *Questions on Doctrine* (this abbreviation will be used from now on for the book, *Seventh-day Adventists Answer Questions on Doctrine*), p. 16.
[34] Froom, *op. cit.*, IV, 845-47.
[35] *Ibid.*, p. 848.
[36] *The Story of our Church*, Prepared by the Department of Education, General Conference of Seventh-day Adventists (Mountain View, Calif.: Pacific Press, 1956), pp. 215-20.
[37] *Ibid.*, pp. 256-61. The *Review and Herald* (full title: *Advent Review and Sabbath Herald*) is the official church paper of the denomination.

After evangelistic work had begun in the western and southern areas of the United States, a period of tremendous foreign expansion began, which was well under way by 1903. Seventh-day Adventist missionaries were sent to Europe, to Africa, to Australia, the South Sea Islands, South America, the Orient, Southern Asia, Central America, and the Middle East.[38] In their Annual Statistical Report for 1971, Seventh-day Adventists claim that they are carrying on work in 189 out of the 226 countries in the world recognized by the United Nations, and that therefore only 37 countries have not yet been entered by them.[39]

The following figures about the membership of the Seventh-day Adventist Church have been culled from the Statistical Report mentioned above, which gives statistics as of December 31, 1971. This document lists a world membership of 2,145,061, and gives the total number of churches as 16,726.[40] If we subtract figures given for the Canadian Union Conference from those given for the North American Division (p. 6), we arrive at the following figures for the United States: 433,906 members and 3,235 churches. It is of particular interest to note that the world membership of the Seventh-day Adventist Church is approximately five times as large as its United States membership; another way of putting this is to say that four out of every five Seventh-day Adventists in the world are to be found outside the United States. These figures, needless to say, point up the tremendous missionary activities of the group.[41]

There are approximately 7,500 ordained ministers in the denomination, and approximately 3,700 licensed ministers.[42] Seventh-day Adventists have 14,896 licensed missionaries on the field, and 6,904 **credentialed missionaries**.[43] There are 48 Seventh-day Adventist Publishing Houses, which publish a total of 282 periodicals.[44] The total

---

[38] *Ibid.*, pp. 267-374.

[39] 109th Annual Statistical Report of Seventh-day Adventists, for the year ending December 31, 1971 (Washington: General Conference of Seventh-day Adventists, 1972), pp. 30-31.

[40] *Ibid.*, p. 20. It is interesting to note that the report lists an increase during 1971 of 221 churches and 98,786 members.

[41] Note that the proportion of foreign churches to churches in the United States is also approximately five to one.

[42] Statistical Report for 1971, p. 21. Licensed ministers may preach but may not administer the sacraments or perform marriage ceremonies.

[43] *Ibid.* Credentialed missionaries are ordained; licensed missionaries are not yet ordained — they may preach but may not administer the sacraments or perform marriage ceremonies.

[44] *Ibid.*, p. 30.

number of languages used in Seventh-day Adventist publications is 167, whereas the total number of languages used in oral work only is 390.[45]

Seventh-day Adventists have an international radio program, *The Voice of Prophecy,* and a nationwide television program, *Faith for Today.* They are very active in educational and medical enterprises. The Statistical Report for 1971 lists 3,934 elementary schools (p. 4), 75 colleges and 379 academies (p. 25), 140 hospitals and sanitariums, 165 clinics and dispensaries, and 49 old people's homes and orphanages (p. 4).

It should be further observed that this movement has experienced a number of splits. The Seventh-day Adventist denomination is the largest and fastest-growing group of Adventists. In an article on "Adventists" in the *Twentieth Century Encyclopedia of Religious Knowledge,* Elmer T. Clark lists six Adventist bodies in addition to the Seventh-day Adventists. Of these the largest is the Advent Christian Church, which in 1951 had a membership of approximately 30,000.

45 *Ibid.,* p. 32.

# II. Source of Authority

The first question we take up as we begin to study the doctrinal teachings of Seventh-day Adventism is that of their source of authority. The main teachings of Seventh-day Adventists are summarized in a set of twenty-two statements entitled "Fundamental Beliefs of Seventh-day Adventists."[46] Article 1 of these *Fundamental Beliefs* reads as follows:

> That the Holy Scriptures of the Old and New Testaments were given by inspiration of God, contain an all-sufficient revelation of His will to men, and are the only unerring rule of faith and practice (2 Tim. 3:15-17).

*Seventh-Day Adventists Answer Questions on Doctrine* is a recent exposition of the teachings of this church, prepared by "a representative group of Seventh-day Adventist leaders, Bible teachers, and editors." The authors explain that the book contains answers to questions which have been raised about Seventh-day Adventist teachings and that these answers are given within the framework of the *Fundamental Beliefs* to which reference has just been made. They add, "In view of this fact, these answers represent the position of our denomination in the area of church doctrine and prophetic interpretation" (p. 8). It is further stated that the officers of the General Conference of Seventh-day Adventists have endorsed this volume, and have recommended it for general use (p. 10). Hence we shall consider this book to be an authentic and reliable source of information about Seventh-day Adventist teach-

[46] These can be found in the *Church Manual*, the *Yearbook*, and also in *Questions on Doctrine*.

22

ings. Let us now note what the authors have to say about the matter of the source of authority:

> Seventh-day Adventists hold the Protestant position that the Bible and the Bible only is the sole rule of faith and practice for Christians. We believe that all theological beliefs must be measured by the living Word, judged by its truth, and whatsoever is unable to pass this test, or is found to be out of harmony with its message, is to be rejected.[47]

So far, therefore, it would appear that Seventh-day Adventists agree with all conservative Protestants in accepting the Bible as the sole rule of faith and life, and as the ultimate source of authority.

When the question is asked: "Do Seventh-day Adventists regard the writings of Ellen G. White as on an equal plane with the writings of the Bible?", the answer given begins as follows:

> 1. That we do not regard the writings of Ellen G. White as an addition to the sacred canon of Scripture.
> 2. That we do not think of them as of universal application, as is the Bible, but particularly for the Seventh-day Adventist Church.
> 3. That we do not regard them in the same sense as the Holy Scriptures, which stand alone and unique as the standard by which all other writings must be judged.[48]

In further explication of this point, the authors of *Questions on Doctrine* go on to say:

> Seventh-day Adventists uniformly believe that the canon of Scripture closed with the book of Revelation. We hold that all other writings and teachings, from whatever source, are to be judged by, and are subject to, the Bible, which is the spring and norm of the Christian faith. We test the writings of Ellen G. White by the Bible, but in no sense do we test the Bible by her writings.[49]

In fact, these authors support their contention by quoting statements from Mrs. White herself, such as the following:

> I recommend to you, dear reader, the Word of God as the rule of your faith and practice. By that Word we are to be judged.[50]

---

[47] *Questions on Doctrine,* p. 28.
[48] *Ibid.,* p. 89.
[49] *Ibid.,* pp. 89-90. To the same effect are statements by Francis D. Nichol, leading Seventh-day Adventist apologist, in *Ellen G. White and her Critics,* pp. 87-90.
[50] *Early Writings,* p. 78; quoted in *Questions on Doctrine,* p. 90.

> Little heed is given to the Bible, and the Lord has given a
> lesser light to lead men and women to the greater light.[51]

As we have previously noted, however, Seventh-day Adventists
do claim that Mrs. White had the gift of prophecy, and that this
gift of prophecy is one of the identifying marks of the remnant
church.[52]  From Revelation 12:17 (in the King James Version)
they gather that this remnant church has "the testimony of Jesus
Christ"; and from Revelation 19:10 they learn that "the testimony
of Jesus is the spirit of prophecy." Since, now, the Spirit of prophecy (at this point, contrary to the King James Version, they capi-
talize the word *spirit*) manifests Himself in the gift of prophecy,
and since, as they believe, Mrs. White had this gift of prophecy,
they conclude that the Seventh-day Adventist denomination must
be the remnant church of which Revelation 12:17 speaks.[53]
Though not placing Mrs. White into the same category as the
writers of the canon of Scripture, the authors of *Questions on Doctrine* compare her to the "prophets or messengers who lived con-
temporaneously with the writers of the two Testaments, but whose
utterances were never a part of Scripture canon."[54]  The Seventh-
day Adventist evaluation of Mrs. White is summed up in the
following words:

> While Adventists hold the writings of Ellen G. White in
> highest esteem, yet these are not the source of our expositions.
> We base our teachings on the Scriptures, the only foundation of
> all true Christian doctrine. However, it is our belief that the
> Holy Spirit opened to her mind important events and called her
> to give certain instructions for these last days. And inasmuch
> as these instructions, in our understanding, are in harmony with
> the Word of God, which Word alone is able to make us wise
> unto salvation, we as a denomination accept them as inspired
> counsels from the Lord.[55]

We are thankful to note that Seventh-day Adventists *claim* that
they do not add any writings to the Sacred Scriptures, and that in
this way, theoretically at least, they distinguish themselves from

[51] *Review and Herald,* Jan. 20, 1903; quoted in *Questions on Doctrine,*
p. 93. The implication is that Mrs. White herself is the "lesser light."
[52] See above, pp. 18-19.
[53] *Questions on Doctrine,* pp. 95-96.
[54] *Ibid.,* pp. 90-91. Among the examples given of this type of person
is John the Baptist. It will be recalled, however, that some of his
utterances did become a part of the canonical Scriptures: e.g., Mt. 3:2,
7-12.
[55] *Ibid.,* p. 93.

a group like the Mormons. It must be said, however, that their use of Mrs. White's writings and their avowed acceptance of her "prophetic gift" are not consistent with this claim. In substantiation of this judgment I offer the following considerations:

(1) Though Seventh-day Adventists claim that they test Mrs. White's writings by the Bible,[56] they assert, on another page of the same volume, that the instructions which she gave the church are in harmony with the Word of God.[57] The latter statement is not qualified in any way; they do not say that *most* of her instructions were in harmony with the Bible, or that her instructions were *generally* in harmony with God's Word — they simply state: "these instructions, in our understanding, are in harmony with the Word of God. . . ." This latter assertion, however, actually nullifies the former. How can one honestly claim to test the writings of a person by the Word of God when one already assumes, as a foregone conclusion, that these writings are in harmony with that Word?

(2) Though Seventh-day Adventists claim to test Mrs. White's writings by the Bible, they call her writings "inspired counsels from the Lord," and say that "the Holy Spirit opened to her mind important events and called her to give certain instructions for these last days."[58] If this is so, however, who may criticize her writings? If they are inspired, they must be true. If her instructions come from the Holy Spirit, they must be true. How, then, could anyone dare to suggest that any of her instructions might be contrary to Scripture? Could messages come from the Holy Spirit which would be contrary to the Word which that same Spirit inspired? Could "inspired counsels from the Lord" be in contradiction to the Lord's Scriptures? Again we must conclude that by describing Mrs. White's instructions as they do, Seventh-day Adventists negate their assertion that they test her writings by the Bible.

(3) Though Seventh-day Adventists claim to test Mrs. White's writings by the Bible, they insist that the gift of prophecy which she possessed, and with which she therefore enriched their group, is a mark of the "remnant church."[59] This means that this gift sets the Seventh-day Adventists apart from all other groups. But

56 *Ibid.*, p. 90.
57 *Ibid.*, p. 93.
58 *Ibid.*
59 *Ibid.*, pp. 95-96. The question of what they understand by this "remnant church" will be taken up in greater detail when we examine their doctrine of the church.

other Christian groups also have the Bible. What, therefore, sets the Seventh-day Adventists apart is what they have in addition to the Bible, namely, the gift of prophecy as manifested in Mrs. White. But if they test Mrs. White's writings by the Bible, as they say, and if the Bible is really their final authority, what do they really have which sets them apart from other groups? It is quite clear at this point that Seventh-day Adventists do not really test Mrs. White's writings by Scripture, but use them alongside of Scripture, and find in their use a mark of distinction which sets them apart from other groups.

(4) Though Seventh-day Adventists claim to test Mrs. White's writings by the Bible, they maintain that these writings "are not of universal application, as is the Bible, but [are] particularly for the Seventh-day Adventist Church."[60] But, we ask, why are they not of universal application? If her writings are tested by Scripture, there should be nothing in them which is contrary to Scripture; if this is so, why should not all her writings be of universal application? Why should not all Christians be bound to accept them, as all Christians are bound to accept the Bible? If her instructions were from the Holy Spirit, why were they not for everyone? Does the Holy Spirit ordinarily work this way? Does He give instructions and counsels for one body of believers only, which are not binding on others? Putting the question another way, if these instructions are not of universal application, are they really from the Holy Spirit? Are they really in perfect agreement with Scripture?

At this point Seventh-day Adventists really claim to have a special source of divine guidance which is not shared by other groups of believers. Is this really much different from the claims of the Mormons?

(5) Though Seventh-day Adventists claim to test Mrs. White's writings by the Bible, their actual usage of her writings nullifies this claim. Instead of testing her writings by the Bible, they use statements from her writings to substantiate their interpretation of Scripture. Typical of their method, for example, is their treatment of the Investigative Judgment, one of the key doctrines of their faith. Under the heading, "Investigative Judgment as Part of the Program of God," the necessity for this investigative judgment (made by Christ before the end of the world) is "proved" by a reference to two passages of Scripture which are ordinarily

60 *Ibid.*, p. 89.

taken to refer to the final judgment at the end of time (Dan. 7:10, and Rev. 20:12). No attempt is made to explain these passages; they are, in fact, not even quoted — a simple reference is considered sufficient. Soon, however, a passage from Mrs. White is quoted in full, to prove that there must be an "investigative judgment" prior to the final judgment:

> There must be an examination of the books of record to determine who, through repentance of sin and faith in Christ, are entitled to the benefits of His atonement. The cleansing of the sanctuary therefore involves a work of investigation — a work of judgment. This work must be performed prior to the coming of Christ to redeem His people; for when He comes, His reward is with Him to give to every man according to his works.[61]

Is this, now, testing Mrs. White's writings by the Bible? Or is this interpreting the Bible by the writings of Mrs. White?

As a matter of fact, Seventh-day Adventists quote more from Mrs. White than from any other author. *Questions on Doctrine* is virtually studded with quotations from Mrs. White. To give an example, Chapter 6 of *Questions on Doctrine,* dealing with "The Incarnation and the 'Son of Man,' " contains the following number of quotations from Mrs. White: one on page 51, one on page 53, two on page 54, five on page 55, one on page 56, four on page 57, one on page 58, three on page 59, ten on page 60, eight on page 61, two on page 62, one on page 63, and two on page 65! The same practice characterizes other Seventh-day Adventist writings. Walter Martin quotes a statement from Wilbur M. Smith which reads in part as follows:

> I do not know any other denomination in all of Christendom today that has given such recognition, so slavishly and exclusively, to its founder or principal theologian as has this commentary [the new Seventh-day Adventist commentary] to the writings of Ellen White. At the conclusion of every chapter in this work is a section headed, "Ellen G. White Comments."[62]

As a further illustration of the actual usage of Mrs. White's writings made by Seventh-day Adventists, I instance their recent

---

[61] *The Great Controversy,* p. 422. The above discussion will be found on pp. 420-422 of *Questions on Doctrine.*
[62] From a letter to Martin, quoted in the latter's *Truth About Seventh-Day Adventism,* pp. 95-96.

publication entitled *Principles of Life from the Word of God*.[63]
This is a textbook on Seventh-day Adventist doctrinal teachings,
intended for classroom use. The method used is that of questions
and answers. Usually the question is answered by a reference to
a passage from the Bible, followed by a quotation from one of
Mrs. White's writings. Frequently, however, no Scripture passage
is given in answer to a question; there is only a quotation from
Mrs. White. One can hardly turn a page of this book without
finding several quotations from Mrs. White; she is virtually the
only authority quoted, alongside of the Bible. Quite in agreement
with the plan of the book, a paragraph from the introductory statement to the student reads as follows:

> This new book, "Principles of Life From the Word of God,"
> has been written for the express purpose of giving you the facts
> upon which to make your everyday decisions and to solve life's
> complex problems. It is written for you. The greater part of
> the evidences cited are from the Bible or the spirit of prophecy
> — our two main sources of divine wisdom.

The expression, "the spirit of prophecy," in the last sentence above
is intended to designate the writings of Mrs. White. When these
writings are thus described as one of their "two main sources of
divine wisdom," are not Seventh-day Adventists actually recog-
nizing Mrs. White's teachings as a second source of authority
alongside of Scripture?

It is also significant to note that nowhere in Adventist literature do we read the admission that Mrs. White may have been in
error on any point of doctrine. Francis D. Nichol, in *Ellen G.
White and her Critics,* goes to great lengths to defend Mrs. White
from various types of charges made against her, but nowhere in
his 703 pages admits that Mrs. White could have been in error
on a doctrinal matter. He does grant in one instance that she
was wrong, but this was not a doctrinal matter; it was, so Nichol
explains, an exercise of private judgment.[64] Does it seem reason-

---

[63] Prepared by the Department of Education of the General Conference
of Seventh-day Adventists, and published by the Pacific Press Publishing
Association of Mountain View, Calif., in 1952. It was reprinted as
recently as 1960.

[64] In the matter of advising the construction of the Battle Creek Health
Reform Institute (pp. 495-504). Martin attacks the assertion that this
was merely a matter of "private judgment," since, so he contends,
the point on which she admitted she was wrong had been introduced with
the formula "I was shown" — the customary way of indicating something which came to her through the "Spirit of prophecy" (*op. cit.,* pp.
105-107).

able to hold that a woman who wrote as many volumes of Scriptural exposition and doctrinal comment as Mrs. White did could never be wrong?

In further substantiation of the point which is being made, I quote from D. M. Canright, who was a Seventh-day Adventist for twenty-eight years, but left the movement because he became convinced that it was in error. Mr. Canright, who was personally acquainted with both Mr. and Mrs. White, and who therefore had first-hand knowledge of the movement, has set forth his objections to Seventh-day Adventism in a volume entitled *Seventh-day Adventism Renounced.*[65] In this book he quotes a statement by Mrs. White in which she equated her writings with those of the prophets and apostles: "In ancient times God spoke to men by the mouth of prophets and apostles. In these days he speaks to them by the Testimonies of his spirit."[66] Canright further quotes a statement from the Advent *Review* of July 2, 1889, to this effect: "We [Seventh-day Adventists] will not neglect the study of the Bible and the *Testimonies.*" He adds the following comment:

> This illustrates the place they assign her [Mrs. White's] writings, viz., an appendix to the Bible. She occupies the same relation to her people that Mrs. Southcott did to hers, Ann Lee to the Shakers, and Joe Smith to the Mormons.[67]

Mr. Canright goes on to say that anyone in the Advent movement who rejects or opposes the "testimonies" of Mrs. White is branded as a rebel fighting against God.[68] He observes:

> There is not a doctrine nor a practice of the church, from the observance of the Sabbath to the washing of feet, upon which she has not written. That settles it. No further investigation can be made on any of these matters, only to gather evidence and construe everything to sustain it. How, then, can their ministers or people be free to think and investigate for themselves? They can not, dare not, and do not.[69]

[65] Originally published in 1889 by Fleming H. Revell, later published by B. C. Goodpasture, and reprinted in 1961 from the 1914 edition by Baker Book House of Grand Rapids.
[66] Testimony No. 33, p. 189; quoted by Canright on p. 135. "Testimonies" was the name commonly given to Mrs. White's specific instructions for the Church.
[67] *Seventh-day Adventism Renounced* (1961 printing), p. 135.
[68] *Ibid.,* p. 135.
[69] *Ibid.,* pp. 136-37.

On a previous page he says:

> Among themselves they [the Seventh-day Adventists] quote
> her [Mrs. White] as we do Paul. A text from her writings is
> an end of all controversy in doctrine and discipline. It is
> common to hear them say that when they give up her visions
> they will give up the Bible too, and they often do.[70]

Is it any wonder, then, that Canright feels compelled to assert:
"Thus they [the Seventh-day Adventists] have another Bible, just
the same as the Mormons have. They have to read our old Bible
in the light of this new Bible."[71]

One can understand, of course, that Mr. Canright would be very
critical of a movement which he himself had left. Even if we
allow for some overstatement in his utterances, however, the statements made by Seventh-day Adventists in their recent doctrinal volume, and the actual use they make of Mrs. White's writings, are
sufficient to establish the conclusion that Seventh-day Adventists
do actually place Mrs. White's writings above the Bible, even while
claiming that they do not. What is really determinative for their
theological position is not careful, objective, scholarly searching
of the Scriptures, but the teachings and visions of Ellen G. White,
which are, for them, the court of final appeal. On the question
of their source of authority, therefore, we must reluctantly insist
that Seventh-day Adventists do not bow before the Scriptures as
their ultimate authority in matters of faith and life.[72]

---

[70] *Ibid.*, p. 135.

[71] *Ibid.*, p. 136.

[72] Needless to say, the relationship of this group to Mrs. White has crucial
bearing on the question, much discussed of late, of whether Seventh-day Adventism is to be considered a cult, or whether it is to be classed with the historic Christian churches. This question is taken up in detail in Chapter 6 of
*The Four Major Cults.*

# III. Doctrines

## DOCTRINE OF GOD

### BEING OF GOD

On the doctrine of the being of God Seventh-day Adventists do not differ from historic Christianity. We are thankful that in this respect they are not at all in the same category as Mormons, Christian Scientists, or Jehovah's Witnesses, all of whom deny the doctrine of the Trinity. Seventh-day Adventists clearly affirm the Trinity, as Article 2 of their *Fundamental Beliefs* reveals:

> That the Godhead, or Trinity, consists of the Eternal Father, a personal, spiritual Being, omnipotent, omnipresent, omniscient, infinite in wisdom and love; the Lord Jesus Christ, the Son of the Eternal Father, through whom all things were created and through whom the salvation of the redeemed hosts will be accomplished; the Holy Spirit, the third person of the Godhead, the great regenerating power in the work of redemption (Mt. 28:19).

It will be noted from this statement that the personality and infinity of God the Father is clearly attested, as well as the personality and full deity of the Holy Spirit. The deity of Jesus Christ, though implied in Article 2, is plainly asserted in Article 3: "That Jesus Christ is very God, being of the same nature and essence as the Eternal Father."

### WORKS OF GOD

*Decrees.* Though Seventh-day Adventists claim that they are neither Calvinist nor totally Arminian in their theology,[73]

73 *Questions on Doctrine,* p. 405.

a careful examination of their writings reveals that they quite definitely reject the Calvinistic view of God's decrees. They explicitly repudiate the position that men "are not all created with a similar destiny; but eternal life is fore-ordained for some, and eternal damnation for others."[74] Their rejection of this statement would seem to imply that they believe that men were all created with a similar destiny, and that the varied destinies of men (the certainty of which they acknowledge) were not in any way foreordained. Their position on this matter, as explicitly stated on another page, is that God foreknew but did not foreordain the salvation of those who are to be saved:

> . . . As our eternal Sovereign God, He is omniscient. He knows the end from the beginning. Even before the creation of the world He knew man would sin and that he would need a Savior. Moreover, as Sovereign God, He also knows just who will accept and who will reject His "great salvation."[75]

In agreement with this, they affirm in an earlier section of the book that they believe "that man is free to choose or reject the offer of salvation through Christ; we do not believe that God has predetermined that some men shall be saved and others lost."[76]

The position, however, that God foreknows who will believe but has not foreordained the actions of men is definitely the Arminian one and not the Calvinistic. It is therefore more accurate to say that Seventh-day Adventists are Arminians on this point than to suggest, as they do, that they stand somewhere between Calvinism and Arminianism.

*Creation.* Seventh-day Adventists believe "that God created the world in six literal days"; they add, "we do not believe that creation was accomplished by long aeons of evolutionary processes."[77] They therefore conduct a vigorous polemic against evolutionary teachings of various sorts, and also against the suggestion that the creative process could have involved long aeons of time.[78]

[74] Calvin, *Institutes*, III, 21, 5; quoted in *Questions on Doctrine*, p. 406. Their discussion of Calvin's position here, restricted as it is to two brief quotations, is quite unsatisfactory, and takes no account of the Reformer's teaching on human responsibility.
[75] *Questions on Doctrine*, p. 420.
[76] *Ibid.*, p. 23.
[77] *Ibid.*, p. 24.
[78] See, for example, Chap. 33 of Wm. H. Branson's *Drama of the Ages* (Washington: Review and Herald, 1950); and pp. 467-89 of Francis Nichol's *Answers to Objections* (Review and Herald, 1952).

*Providence.* Belief in Divine Providence is clearly expressed by Seventh-day Adventists: ". . . God is the Sovereign Creator, upholder, and ruler of the universe, and He is eternal, omnipotent, omniscient, and omnipresent."[79]

## DOCTRINE OF MAN

### MAN IN HIS ORIGINAL STATE

*The Creation of Man.* Seventh-day Adventists accept fully the Genesis account of the creation of man. In agreement with Genesis 1:26 they teach that man was created in the image of God. Carlyle B. Haynes, one of their writers, explains what is involved in the image of God: man had a free will, the power of intelligent action, the authority to exercise dominion on the earth, and the faculty of knowing, loving, and obeying his Creator.[80]

*The Constitutional Nature of Man.* Seventh-day Adventists are very critical of the commonly held conception that man consists of two aspects — a physical aspect called *body,* and a nonphysical aspect called *soul* or *spirit.* Since their views on this matter have reference both to the constitutional nature of man and to the question of man's existence after death, we shall begin examining their teachings on this subject at this point, but shall return to them when we come to their doctrine of the last things.

In *Questions on Doctrine* (p. 23) we read the following: ". . . Man was endowed at creation with conditional immortality; we do not believe that man has innate immortality or an immortal soul." To know what Seventh-day Adventists understand by the term *soul,* we must turn to their answer to Question 40 in the above-named book. On the basis of studies of both the Hebrew word *nephesh* and the Greek word *psuchee,* as these occur in the Bible, the authors of this volume conclude that there is nothing in the use of either of these words which implies a conscious entity that can survive the death of the body.[81] They insist that *soul* in the Bible refers to the individual rather than to a constituent

[79] *Questions on Doctrine,* pp. 21-22. Cf. Nichol, *Answers to Objections* p. 457.
[80] *Life, Death, and Immortality* (Nashville: Southern Publishing Association, 1952), p. 49.
[81] *Questions on Doctrine,* pp. 512-14.

part of the individual, and that it is therefore more accurate to say that a certain person *is* a soul than to say that he *has* a soul.[82] "The Scriptures teach," the authors summarize, "that the soul of man represents the whole man, and not a particular part independent of the other component parts of man's nature; and further, that the soul cannot exist apart from the body, for man is a unit."[83]

What these authors are driving at is that, in their judgment, there is no soul which survives after the body dies. This point is made crystal-clear by Carlyle Haynes. Taking his point of departure from Genesis 2:7 ("The Lord God formed man of the dust of the ground, and breathed into his nostrils the breath of life; and man became a living soul," KJ), Haynes says:

> The union of two things, earth and breath, served to create a third thing, soul. The continued existence of the soul depended wholly upon the continued union of breath and body. When that union is broken and the breath separates from the body, as it does at death, the soul ceases to exist.[84]

The authors of *Questions on Doctrine* also discuss the word *spirit* as it occurs in the Bible. After giving a brief word study of the Hebrew word *ruach* and the Greek word *pneuma,* they conclude that neither word ever denotes a separate entity capable of conscious existence apart from the physical body.[85] The conclusion of their study of this matter is: "Seventh-day Adventists do not believe that the whole man or any part of him is inherently immortal."[86]

### MAN IN THE STATE OF SIN

*The Fall.* Seventh-day Adventists teach "that man was created sinless, but by his subsequent fall entered a state of alienation and depravity."[87]

*Original Sin.* It is held by this group that the results of Adam's sin were transmitted to all succeeding generations.

> Sin . . . is an inheritance. Men are born sinners. Through disobedience, Adam's nature became changed. He was no longer a holy and righteous being, but a sinful being. And this

---

82 *Ibid.,* p. 513.
83 *Ibid.,* p. 515.
84 *Op. cit.,* p. 54.
85 Pp. 515-17.
86 *Ibid.,* p. 518.
87 *Ibid.,* p. 22.

sinful nature must, of necessity, be transmitted to his children as an inheritance.[88]

Branson further comments that to this inherited sin Adam's posterity have added the guilt of their own transgressions. Seventh-day Adventists thus distinguish, in common with most Christian churches, between original sin and actual sin.

When the question is asked, What effect does this sinful nature have on man's ability to accept salvation through Christ, it is difficult to find an unambiguous answer. On the one hand, Seventh-day Adventism teaches that man is dead in sin, and that therefore even the initial promptings to a better life must come from God.[89] On the other hand, it affirms "that man is free to choose or reject the offer of salvation through Christ. . . ."[90] Putting these two statements together, we conclude that initial promptings to a better life must come, somehow, to every man, or at least to every man who hears the gospel, and that then man must make his own choice as to what he will do in response to these promptings. The decisive factor in determining who will be saved is thus not God's sovereign grace but man's free choice. The position of Seventh-day Adventism on this point would again appear to be basically the Arminian one.[91]

## DOCTRINE OF CHRIST

### THE PERSON OF CHRIST

*Deity of Christ.* As has been stated, Seventh-day Adventists unequivocally affirm the full deity of Jesus Christ. Their view of Christ is summarized in Article 3 of their *Fundamental Beliefs*:

> That Jesus Christ is very God, being of the same nature and essence as the Eternal Father. While retaining His divine nature He took upon Himself the nature of the human family, lived on the earth as a man, exemplified in His life as our

[88] Branson, *op. cit.*, p. 43.
[89] *Questions on Doctrine*, p. 107.
[90] *Ibid.*, p. 23.
[91] Arminians teach that there is a universal or common grace which comes to all men, enabling them, if they wish, to accept Christ. That this is the teaching of Seventh-day Adventism is shown by the following explanation: "Christ is the true light, who 'lighteth every man that cometh into the world' (Jn. 1:9). This light, in some way known only to Divine Providence, penetrates the darkness of human hearts and kindles the first spark of desire after God. If the soul begins to seek for God then 'the Father which hath sent me [Christ]' will 'draw him [the seeker] (Jn. 6:44)" (*Ibid.*, pp. 107-8).

example the principles of righteousness, attested His relationship to God by many mighty miracles, died for our sins on the
cross, was raised from the dead, and ascended to the Father,
where He ever lives to make intercession for us.

Note that the incarnation of Christ is clearly asserted, that His
miracles are recognized, that His substitutionary death, resurrection, ascension, and intercession are all affirmed. So far there
would appear to be no difference between their teachings and
those of historic Christianity.

Seventh-day Adventists do apply the Biblical name Michael
not to a created angel, but to the Son of God in His pre-incarnate
state;[92] they thus distinguish themselves from the Mormons, who
find in the name Michael a designation for the pre-existent Adam.
Though some earlier Adventist writers had contended that the
Son was not wholly equal to the Father, and that the former must
have had a beginning in the remote past (a form of Arianism), the
denomination today officially affirms Christ's complete equality
with the Father and the pre-existence of the Son from eternity.[93]

*The Human Nature of Christ.* According to many writers,
Seventh-day Adventists teach that, in becoming incarnate, Christ
assumed a polluted human nature. This allegation is made, for
example, by John H. Gerstner in his *Theology of the Major
Sects* (p. 127), and he adds some quotations to support his
charge. Walter Martin, however, contends that Seventh-day
Adventists have now repudiated this position, that one must consider *Questions on Doctrine* as giving their latest statement on
this point, and that anyone who continues to make this charge
is unfair to them, since he is using outdated sources.[94] What
shall we say about this matter?

If one reads carefully pages 53-64 of *Questions on Doctrine,* one
gathers that the authors of this volume definitely wish to remove
the impression that, according to Seventh-day Adventist teaching,
Christ assumed a polluted human nature. A great many quotations
from Mrs. White are cited, both on these pages and in an Appendix
at the back of the book, to prove that Mrs. White really meant
to say not that Christ possessed a sinful human nature, but that
He assumed a human nature which had been weakened by sin.
Statements from Mrs. White are quoted to the effect that, though

[92] *Ibid.,* pp. 71-83.
[93] *Ibid.,* pp. 46-49.
[94] *The Truth About Seventh-day Adventism,* pp. 86-88.

Christ took upon Himself man's nature in its fallen condition, He did not in the least participate in its sin, and that we should have no misgivings in regard to the perfect sinlessness of the human nature of Christ.[95] Another one of Mrs. White's statements is: "Do not set Him [Christ] before the people as a man with the propensities of sin. . . . He could have sinned; He could have fallen, but not for one moment was there in Him an evil propensity."[96] It should be observed here that Christian theologians have usually insisted that we must not say that Christ could have sinned. Yet we here face the question of the reality of Christ's temptation. Though I believe that it is more proper to say that Christ could not sin than to suggest that He could have sinned, the real difficulty with Adventist teaching does not lie here.

In spite of the laudable attempt on the part of the authors of *Questions on Doctrine* to eliminate all ambiguity on this matter, there remain some real difficulties on the question of the sinlessness of Christ's human nature. One of these difficulties is that Mrs. White's teaching was not consistent on this point. Both on page 61 and on page 654 of *Questions on Doctrine* the following statement of Mrs. White is quoted with approval: "He [Christ] took upon His sinless nature our sinful nature."[97] If we analyze this statement, we conclude that, according to Mrs. White, Christ assumed in addition to His divine, sinless nature a human nature which was sinful. Yet this is precisely what Mrs. White is said not to have taught. Would it not be far better for Seventh-day Adventists to admit that Mrs. White was in error when she made this statement?

A further difficulty is that there exist a number of statements by Seventh-day Adventist authors clearly asserting that Christ inherited tendencies to sin. One of the best known is the statement by L. A. Wilcox to the effect that Christ conquered over sin "in spite of bad blood and an inherited meanness."[98] Though the discussion of this matter in *Questions on Doctrine* implies that the denomination would now repudiate this statement, nowhere

[95] *Questions on Doctrine*, p. 659. The quotation is from *Signs of the Times*, June 9, 1898.
[96] *Questions on Doctrine*, p. 651. The quotation is from the *Seventh-day Adventist Bible Commentary*, V, 1128.
[97] From *Medical Ministry*, p. 181.
[98] From *Signs of the Times*, March, 1927; quoted by Martin, *op. cit.*, p. 86.

in the book are we definitely told that this has been done. Further, in 1950 William Henry Branson, who served from 1950 to 1954 as President of the General Conference of Seventh-day Adventists, published a book entitled *Drama of the Ages.* In this book, which can certainly not be called an "outdated source," the following statement occurs:

> The Catholic doctrine of the "immaculate conception" is that Mary, the mother of our Lord, was preserved from original sin. If this be true, then Jesus did not partake of man's sinful nature (p. 101).

The author clearly indicates that he does not deem this Catholic doctrine to be true. It then follows that, in his judgment, Jesus *did* partake of man's sinful nature. We find no indication in *Questions on Doctrine* that this recent statement has been repudiated by the denomination. On the question, therefore, of the sinlessness of Christ's human nature, we conclude that there is still much ambiguity in Seventh-day Adventist teaching.[99]

### THE WORK OF CHRIST

*The Atonement of Christ.* Seventh-day Adventists teach the vicarious, substitutionary atonement of Christ. In Article 8 of the *Fundamental Beliefs* their position is set forth as follows:

> The law cannot save the transgressor from his sin, nor impart power to keep him from sinning. In infinite love and mercy, God provides a way whereby this may be done. He furnishes a substitute, even Christ the Righteous One, to die in man's stead, making "him to be sin for us, who knew no sin; that we might be made the righteousness of God in him" (2 Cor. 5:21).

To the same effect is the following statement from *Questions on Doctrine*: ". . . The vicarious, atoning death of Jesus Christ, once for all, is all-sufficient for the redemption of a lost race" (p. 22). Crystal-clear is the summary found in the same volume (p. 396):

> We take our stand without qualification on the gospel platform that the death of Jesus Christ provides the *sole* propitiation for our sins; that there is salvation through no other means or medium, and no other name by which we may be saved: and that the shed blood of Jesus Christ *alone* brings remission for our sins.

[99] This question is carefully and competently treated in Chap. 4 of Herbert S. Bird's *Theology of Seventh-day Adventism* (Grand Rapids: Eerdmans, 1961). This volume is, in fact, one of the ablest evaluations of Seventh-day Adventist doctrines which has appeared.

On the question of the extent of the atonement, their position is clearly the Arminian one: Christ died not just for the elect, but for everyone. ". . . We believe that the sacrificial atonement was made on the cross and was *provided* for all men, but that in the heavenly priestly ministry of Christ our Lord, this sacrificial atonement is *applied* to the seeking soul."[100]

**At this point we must raise a question which is often raised;** it is an important one for a proper understanding of Seventh-day Adventist teachings: Was the atonement finished on the cross? When one reads Seventh-day Adventist literature, one frequently comes across statements to the effect that the atonement was not completed on the cross, that the atonement is still going on, or that there will be a final atonement after Christ's work on the cross. Note, for example, the following quotations from Mrs. White:

> Today He [Christ] is making an atonement for us before the Father.[101]
> Now, while our great High Priest is making the atonement for us, we should seek to become perfect in Christ.[102]
> The blood of Christ, while it was to release the repentant sinner from the condemnation of the law, was not to cancel the sin; it would stand on record in the sanctuary until the final atonement. . . .[103]
> Attended by heavenly angels, our great High Priest enters the holy of holies, and there appears in the presence of God, to engage in the last acts of His ministration in behalf of man, — to perform the work of investigative judgment, and to make an atonement for all who are shown to be entitled to its benefits.[104]

The authors of *Questions on Doctrine* attribute this way of speaking about the atonement to the fact that earlier Adventist writers had a wider conception of the word atonement than do most Christian theologians today. These earlier writers, so it is said, wished to understand the word atonement as applying not just to the sacrifice of Christ once made on the cross, but also to the application of that atonement to sinners. It is in the latter

---

[100] *Questions on Doctrine,* p. 348.
[101] *Manuscript 21, 1895;* quoted in *Questions on Doctrine,* p. 685.
[102] *The Great Controversy Between Christ and Satan* (Mountain View: Pacific Press, 1911), p. 623.
[103] *Patriarchs and Prophets* (Mountain View: Pacific Press, 1913), p. 357.
[104] *The Great Controversy,* p. 480.

sense that we are to understand expressions like those cited above.[105]

When, therefore, one hears an Adventist say, or reads in Adventist literature — even in the writings of Ellen G. White — that Christ is making atonement now, it should be understood that we mean simply that Christ is now making application of the benefits of the sacrificial atonement He made on the cross; that He is making it efficacious for us individually, according to our needs and requests.[106]

The difficulty with the above explanation, however, is that Mrs. White had a sufficiently adequate command of the English language to be able to say "applying atonement" instead of "making atonement." Seventh-day Adventists, by an explanation like the one reproduced above, are introducing confusion into our theological terminology. In the statement about the atonement on page 22 of *Questions on Doctrine* it is said that the vicarious, atoning death of Christ is sufficient for the redemption of a lost race. Here the word atoning obviously does not mean what Christ did after His death on the cross, but refers to what He did on the cross. Why confuse the issue by suggesting that this word may have an additional meaning?

The real reason why Seventh-day Adventists speak of Christ's present work as being a work of atonement lies in their seeing in the heavenly ministry of Christ since 1844 a fulfillment of what was done in Old Testament times by the high priest on the great Day of Atonement. Since what the priest did on that day was an atonement, it is assumed by them that they may speak of what Christ is doing now in the heavenly holy of holies as an atonement. This brings up the question of Seventh-day Adventist teachings on the investigative judgment, to which we now turn.

*The Investigative Judgment.* It will be recalled that reference was made above to O. R. L. Crosier's *Day-Star* article of February 7, 1846, in which the groundwork for the doctrine of the investigative judgment was laid.[107] Later Adventist writers, including particularly Mrs. White, built upon this foundation the doctrine of the investigative judgment. That is, what Crosier called "the process of blotting out sin" — which, he said, Christ began on October 22, 1844, when He entered the holy of holies of the heavenly sanctuary — was called by later Adventists a process of

---

[105] *Questions on Doctrine,* pp. 341-48.
[106] *Ibid.,* pp. 354-55.
[107] Above, pp. 13-14.

judgment, or of investigative judgment. On the cross, it was said, Christ brought the sacrifice whereby atonement was *provided;* after His ascension, He *applied* this sacrifice. This work of application, again, had two phases. From the time of His ascension to October 22, 1844, Christ did a work comparable to the daily ministry of the Old Testament priests, which resulted in the forgiveness of sin but not in the blotting out of sin. At the latter date, however, Christ entered upon the "judgment phase" of His ministry whereby He blots out sin — a work comparable to that of the high priest on the Day of Atonement.[108]

Seventh-day Adventists devote two of their twenty-two *Fundamental Beliefs* to the investigative judgment. After having said that the true sanctuary, of which the tabernacle on earth was a type, is the temple of God in heaven, and that the priestly work of Christ is the antitype (or fulfillment) of the work done by Jewish priests in the earthly sanctuary, Article 14 of the *Fundamental Beliefs* goes on to assert:

> . . . this heavenly sanctuary is the one to be cleansed at the end of the 2300 days of Daniel 8:14, its cleansing being, as in the type, a work of judgment, beginning with the entrance of Christ as the high priest upon the judgment phase of His ministry in the heavenly sanctuary, foreshadowed in the earthly service of cleansing the sanctuary on the day of atonement.

Article 16 describes the work of the investigative judgment in greater detail:

> . . . The time of the cleansing of the sanctuary, synchronizing with the period of the proclamation of the message of Revelation 14, is a time of investigative judgment; first, with reference to the dead, and second, with reference to the living. This investigative judgment determines who of the myriads sleeping in the dust of the earth are worthy of a part in the first resurrection, and who of its living multitudes are worthy of translation (I Peter 4:17, 18; Dan. 7:9, 10; Rev. 14:6, 7; Lk. 20:35).[109]

What, now, does this investigative judgment mean? During this time of judgment, which began in 1844 and is still going on, the names of all professing believers who have ever lived are brought up, beginning with those who first lived on this earth.

---

[108] *Questions on Doctrine,* p. 389.
[109] The *Fundamental Beliefs* can be found on pp. 11-18 of *Questions on Doctrine.*

When a name has been singled out, that person's life is carefully
scrutinized.  The "books" mentioned in Revelation 20:12 ("and
books were opened") are assumed to be books of record, in which
both the good deeds and the bad deeds of every man have been
recorded.  These records are carefully examined.[110]

Christ now acts as the Advocate of His people, pleading cases
which have been committed to Him.  When the name of a true
child of God comes up in the judgment, the record will reveal
that every sin has been confessed and forgiven, and that the individual concerned has tried to keep all of God's commandments.
Such an individual will then be "passed" in the investigative judgment; it will then have been determined that this person is worthy
of a part in the first resurrection.[111]  It is, of course, to be expected
that not all professing believers will pass this test.

An important point to note here is the distinction Seventh-day
Adventists make between the forgiveness of sins and the blotting
out of sins.[112]  When a man repents and believes, so they teach,
his sins are forgiven, but not yet blotted out.  His "forgiven" sins
are still on record in the heavenly sanctuary, even after he has
confessed them and after they have been forgiven.  This, they
contend, is what was taught us by the Old Testament typology:
when the priests brought the blood of the sin-offerings into the
holy place, they simply transferred the iniquities of the people to
the sanctuary.  Taking their cue from the Parable of the Unmerciful Servant in Matthew 18:23-35, Seventh-day Adventists
teach that one's forgiveness can be cancelled after it has been
bestowed, as was the case with the unmerciful servant.  Note the
following statement from *Questions on Doctrine*:

> The actual blotting out of sin, therefore, could not take place
> the moment when a sin is forgiven, because subsequent deeds
> and attitudes may affect the final decision.  Instead, the sin

---

[110] *Questions on Doctrine,* pp. 435-38.  It is not made clear, however, who
examines these records.  From the fact that this is called the judgment
phase of Christ's ministry, one would gather that Christ is the examiner.
Christ is, however, as we shall see, called the Advocate who pleads the
cases of His people.  If He is the Advocate in the investigative judgment,
why should this aspect of Christ's work be called the "judgment phase"
of His ministry?  One senses at this point a basic confusion in Adventist
thought between the work of Christ as priest and His work as judge.

[111] *Ibid.,* pp. 441-42.

[112] It will be remembered that Crosier had already made this distinction.
See above, p. 14.

remains on the record until the life is complete — in fact, the Scriptures indicate it remains until the judgment.[113]

This leads us to the next question: if the sins of a believer are only forgiven when he repents but are not then blotted out, when are his sins blotted out? To this question we get an ambiguous answer. On the one hand it is clear that the sins of believers will not be blotted out until their names have come up in the investigative judgment. This will not happen until after they have lived their lives, so that all their deeds may be taken into consideration. In fact, so Adventists teach, one cannot even say that a man's record is closed when he comes to the end of his days:

> He is responsible for his influence during life, and is just as surely responsible for his evil influence after he is dead. To quote the words of the poet, "The evil that men do lives after them," leaving a trail of sin to be charged to the account. In order to be just, it would seem that God would need to take all these things into account in the judgment.[114]

On the basis of this last statement, it appears that the investigative judgment will not take place until a considerable time after a person's death.[115] When a believer has been accepted by God in the investigative judgment, his sins are no longer held against him.

Some Seventh-day Adventist statements give one the impression that the blotting out of sin occurs when one has been accepted in the investigative judgment. This is the conclusion one draws from the following assertion:

> When He [Christ] confesses before God and the holy angels that the repentant sinner is clothed in the robe of His own spotless character . . . no one in the universe can deny to that saved man an entrance into the eternal kingdom of righteousness. Then, of course, is the time for his sins to be blotted out forever.[116]

*Satan as the Scapegoat.* It becomes apparent from other Adventist statements, however, that one cannot really say that the sins of the person described above have been totally blotted out

---

[113] P. 441. See pp. 439-41.
[114] *Questions on Doctrine*, p. 420.
[115] From Article 16 of the *Fundamental Beliefs*, quoted above, we learn, however, that the investigative judgment of those believers who will still be living when Christ returns to earth will have been completed before the Second Coming, so that they may be translated to glory when the millennium begins.
[116] *Questions on Doctrine*, p. 442.

when he has been accepted in the investigative judgment. These sins still have some sort of existence. They will not really be blotted out until the time of the "final eradication" or "final blotting out" of sin, which will occur just before Christ's return to earth, and will consist in the placing of the sins of all men, both righteous and wicked, on Satan. Let us listen to Mrs. White on this:

> When Christ, by virtue of His own blood, removes the sins of His people from the heavenly sanctuary at the close of His ministration [the investigative judgment], He will place them upon Satan, who, in the execution of the judgment, must bear the final penalty.[117]

> When the investigative judgment closes, Christ will come, and His reward will be with Him to give to every man as his work shall be. . . . As the priest, in removing the sins from the sanctuary, confessed them upon the head of the scapegoat, so Christ will place all these sins upon Satan, the originator and instigator of sin. The scapegoat, bearing the sins of Israel, was sent away . . .; so Satan, bearing the guilt of all the sins which he has caused God's people to commit, will be for a thousand years confined to the earth . . . and he will at last suffer the full penalty of sin in the fires that shall destroy all the wicked. Thus the great plan of redemption will reach its accomplishment in the final eradication of sin. . . .[118]

These statements leave us with no choice but that of concluding that, according to the prophetess of Seventh-day Adventism, sin is not really eradicated from this earth until it has been laid on Satan.

Another Seventh-day Adventist writer specifically calls this transaction with Satan the "final blotting out of sin":

> The final service, in the second apartment [of the tabernacle], on the Day of Atonement, symbolized the concluding judgment-hour phase of Christ's ministry, preparatory to the final blotting out of sin. . . . And the scapegoat . . . symbolized Satan, the instigator of sin, who after the atonement was finished through the substitutionary sacrifice, bears his share of responsibility for all sins, and is banished at last into the abyss of oblivion.[119]

The Froom statement suggests that Satan will bear his share of responsibility, not just for the sins of believers, but for all sins.

117 *The Great Controversy*, p. 422.
118 *Ibid.,* pp. 485-86.
119 Froom, *Prophetic Faith of our Fathers,* IV, 898-99.

The same thought is found on page 400 of *Questions on Doctrine*. All sins, not just the sins of God's people, will thus be laid on him by Christ. And only in this way will sin finally be blotted out of God's universe.

Seventh-day Adventists derive this teaching from their interpretation of the second goat of Leviticus 16. This chapter describes the ritual of the Day of Atonement. Two goats were to be brought to the high priest; he, in turn, was to cast lots upon the goats: "one lot for Jehovah, and the other lot for Azazel" (Lev. 16:8; the King James Version has "for the scapegoat"). After the high priest had completed the work of bringing the blood of the slain first goat into the holy of holies, he laid both of his hands upon the second goat, and then proceeded to confess over him all the sins of the people of Israel. The second goat was then sent away· into the wilderness. Seventh-day Adventists interpret the word Azazel used in this chapter (the Hebrew word translated *scapegoat*) as meaning Satan. They maintain further that this ceremony typified what will happen to Satan at the end of time:

> One [goat] typified our Lord and Savior Jesus Christ, who was slain as our substitute and vicariously bore our sins with all the guilt and punishment entailed. . . . The other goat, we believe, stood for Satan, who is eventually to have rolled back upon his own head, not only his own sins, but the responsibility for all the sins he has caused others to commit.[120]

These authors go on to make a point of the fact that the live goat was not slain, and therefore did not provide any propitiation for the sins of the people. So, they continue,

> Satan makes no atonement for our sins. But Satan will ultimately have to bear the retributive punishment for his responsibility in the sins of all men, both righteous and wicked.[121]

Seventh-day Adventists therefore completely repudiate the suggestion that Satan is in any sense our sin-bearer, or that he makes atonement for our sins in any way. Christ, so they say, is the only one who made atonement for our sins.[122] Yet they contend

---

[120] *Questions on Doctrine,* p. 399.
[121] *Ibid.,* p. 400·
[122] It must not be forgotten, however, that Adventists use the word atonement in an ambiguous way. Mrs. White even said, it will be recalled, that the blood of Christ did not cancel the sin of the penitent, but that

that sin is not completely eradicated from the earth until all sin has been laid on Satan.

Summarizing, we must say that the Seventh-day Adventist view of the atonement of Christ contains conflicting emphases. While insisting, along with all evangelical Christians, that the vicarious death of Christ was sufficient for the redemption of a lost race, they have supplemented this pivotal doctrine of historic Christianity with their teachings on the investigative judgment and the placing of sins on Satan. While wishing to maintain that men are saved by grace alone, Seventh-day Adventists have cast a shadow over that claim by their views on the investigative judgment, since they assert that it is this judgment, with its examination of man's life and work, which *determines* whether a person shall be saved or not. The investigative-judgment doctrine impugns the sovereignty of God, since it implies that neither God the Father nor Christ knows who are truly God's people until after this examination has been concluded. The distinction between the forgiveness of sins and the blotting out of sins which Seventh-day Adventists make jeopardizes the security of the child of God, and makes it impossible for anyone to know, even in the hour of his death, whether he is saved or not. And the conception that the sins of all men are to be laid on Satan assigns to Satan an indispensable role in the blotting out of sin, thus detracting from the all-sufficiency of Christ.

A more detailed evaluation of Seventh-day Adventist teachings on the investigative judgment and on Satan as the scapegoat will be found in Appendix A.[123]

## DOCTRINE OF SALVATION

### JUSTIFICATION AND SANCTIFICATION

How is man saved, according to Seventh-day Adventism? At first glance, their position looks very sound.

---

this sin would stand on record in the sanctuary until the *final atonement* (see above, p. 39, n. 103).

[123] Able treatments of these teachings will be found in Chap. 5 of Bird's *Theology of Seventh-day Adventism*, and in Chap. 9 of Norman F. Douty's *Another Look at Seventh-day Adventism* (Grand Rapids: Baker, 1962).

> . . . That which saves is grace alone, through faith in the living Christ. And similarly, that which justifies is His free and blessed grace. We likewise believe in works, and in full obedience to the will and commandments of God. But the works in which we believe, and that we seek to perform, are the result, or fruitage, of salvation, not a means to salvation, in whole or in part. And the obedience that we render is the loving response of a life that is saved by grace. Salvation is never earned; it is a gift from God through Jesus Christ.[124]

What about justification? It is defined as follows: "When we accept Him [Christ] we are justified. That is, His righteousness is imputed to us, and we stand before God just as though we had never sinned."[125] In Article 8 of the *Fundamental Beliefs* we read: ". . . one is justified, not by obedience to the law, but by the grace that is in Christ Jesus." Note also the following statement: "We cannot be justified at all by any kind of works. Justification is wholly an act of God, and we are but the recipients of His unbounded grace."[126] So far it would appear that Seventh-day Adventist soteriology is basically the same as that of Calvin and Luther.

What about sanctification? It is difficult to find a single, clear definition of sanctification in *Questions on Doctrine*. On page 23 we are told "that man is sanctified by the indwelling Christ through the Holy Spirit." From page 410 we learn that, whereas the first work of grace is justification, the continuing work of grace is sanctification. From page 388 we gather that ". . . while justification is *imputed* righteousness, sanctification is *imparted* righteousness." So far the statements quoted have pictured sanctification as a work of God. Man's responsibility in his own sanctification, however, is stressed in the following words from page 387:

> While Christ is "made unto us wisdom, and righteousness, and sanctification, and redemption" (I Cor. 1:30), yet the only ones who are perfected or sanctified are those who fully accept of His grace. . . . When we accept Him we are justified. . . . But only those who follow on and experience Him as an indwelling power, and who continually appropriate His grace for victory over their sinful natures, are sanctified or perfected.

---

[124] *Questions on Doctrine*, p. 102. Cf. p. 108.
[125] *Ibid.*, p. 387.
[126] *Ibid.*, p. 116.

It is thus clear that man must continually appropriate God's grace and experience Christ's indwelling power in order to be sanctified.

The word *perfected* in the above quotation puzzles the non-Adventist reader. The statement could be read so as to teach that sanctification means sinless perfection, and to imply that unless one has attained such a state, he has not really been sanctified. Do Seventh-day Adventists teach this? One does not find a clear answer to this question in *Questions on Doctrine*. On the one hand, their insistence that Christians must confess every sin, and that these confessions of sin will play an important part in the investigative judgment, leads one to think that they do not envision sinless perfection as possible on this earth. On the other hand, by applying to themselves as a group the words of Revelation 12:17, "which keep the commandments of God," they seem to imply that they are actually keeping God's commandments perfectly, in distinction from other groups.

Though they are not clear on this point, it does not appear that Seventh-day Adventists are perfectionists. The writings of Mrs. White teach that the last vestiges of sin will not be removed from man until the resurrection from the dead has occurred. A very striking exception to this rule, however, is found in Seventh-day Adventist teachings about the so-called "time of trouble." M. L. Andreasen, in his book, *The Sanctuary Service,* maintains that the last generation of Christians on the old earth will live completely without sin, and thus give a final demonstration of what God can do with humanity.[127] Making frequent use of Revelation 14:12 ("Here is the patience of the saints; here are they that keep the commandments of God . . .," KJ), Mr. Andreasen claims that this last generation is the group spoken of in the Bible as the 144,000 (p. 315). He contends, in fact, that in this final demonstration men will follow the example of Christ Himself and "prove that what God did in Christ, He can do in every human being who submits to Him" (p. 299). According to this author, therefore, it will be possible for at least one generation of men to live lives as sinless as that of Jesus Christ!

It should further be stated at this point that Seventh-day Adventists decisively reject the doctrine of eternal security, namely,

---

[127] P. 302. I quote from the 2nd ed., published by Review and Herald Pub. Ass'n in 1947. This teaching is, however, also found in the writings of Mrs. White. See *The Great Controversy,* pp. 425, 613-14, and 623; cf. Douty's discussion of this point in *op. cit.,* pp. 74-75.

that if one has once been regenerated and justified, he cannot fall away from grace in such a way as to be lost. It will be recalled that, according to *Questions on Doctrine* (p. 441), the actual blotting out of sin cannot take place the moment a sin is forgiven, because subsequent deeds and attitudes may affect the final decision. The expression, "subsequent deeds," tells us that by doing wrong deeds a person may lose the forgiveness he has received — which forgiveness would, we take it, be tantamount to justification. To the same effect is the following statement: commenting on Ezekiel 18:20-24, the authors of *Questions on Doctrine* affirm,

> In these verses, two men are brought to view. The one, a wicked man who turns from his sin and becomes obedient to God. He is forgiven; and if he walks in the way of righteousness, none of his former sins will ever be mentioned unto him. The other, a righteous man who turns from the path of righteousness, and goes back into sin. If he continues in iniquity, none of his previous manifestations of goodness will ever be mentioned. He forfeits all the blessings of salvation and goes down into death (p. 415).

The last sentence clearly suggests that this man did have salvation, but has now lost it.

Seventh-day Adventists thus teach that, though one is justified by grace alone, through believing in Christ and having His righteousness imputed to us, it is possible for a person, through subsequent sinful deeds and attitudes, to lose this justification and still be eternally lost. This would imply that the only way one can be sure of retaining his justification is to continue to do the right kind of deeds and maintain the right attitudes throughout the rest of his life. It will be granted, of course, that, according to Adventists, one can only do these deeds and maintain these attitudes through divine grace. But the question now arises: when we look at salvation in its totality, is this salvation for the Seventh-day Adventist due to God's grace alone, or is it due partly to God's grace and partly to man's faithfulness in keeping God's commandments? It is this point which we must now examine more closely.

## THE QUESTION OF LEGALISM

Harold Lindsell has contended that the Seventh-day Adventists are guilty of the error of "Galatianism" — that is, that man is saved partly by the work of Christ and partly by the keeping of the law. He bases this conclusion particularly upon their teachings about the keeping of the Sabbath Day. He supports his contention by quoting the following statement from page 449 of Mrs. White's *Great Controversy*:

> . . . In the last days the Sabbath test will be made plain. When this time comes anyone who does not keep the Sabbath will receive the mark of the beast and will be kept from heaven.[128]

After making further quotations from Seventh-day Adventist writings, including *Questions on Doctrine,* Lindsell summarizes as follows: ". . . If men now or later must keep the Sabbath to demonstrate their salvation or to prevent their being lost, then grace is no more grace. Rather, we are saved by grace and kept by works."[129]

Mr. Lindsell's charge, therefore, is that the Seventh-day Adventists are guilty of a kind of legalism — not the extreme kind, in which one would claim to be saved wholly by his keeping of the law, but a mixed kind, in which one teaches that he is saved by grace but kept by works. The same type of charge is made by Herbert S. Bird, only he bases it on the doctrine of the investigative judgment. He cites a statement by William Branson: "A Christian who through faith in Jesus Christ has faithfully kept the law's requirements will be acquitted; there is no condemnation, for the law finds no fault in him."[130] Bird concludes that, for Seventh-day Adventism, it is the keeping of the commandments that constitutes the sinner's title to heaven — "his keeping of them through faith in Jesus Christ, to be sure, but his keeping of them none the less."[131] And on the last page of his book he expresses the judgment that the "sanctuary position" of this movement "evinces a notion of the way of salvation which is considerably less than all of grace. And we have Paul's word for it that if it be so, it is not of grace at all."[132]

It is my conviction that the charges made by Lindsell and Bird are valid, and that Seventh-day Adventists, though they claim to teach salvation by grace alone, are guilty of the kind of mixed legalism to which these writers point. I base this conviction on the following grounds:

(1) *The doctrine of the investigative judgment.* We appreciate

---

[128] "What of Seventh-day Adventism?", *Christianity Today,* April 14. 1958, p. 13.
[129] *Ibid.,* p. 15.
[130] *Drama of the Ages,* p. 351; quoted in Bird, *op. cit.,* p. 90.
[131] Bird, *op. cit.,* p. 90.
[132] *Ibid.,* p. 132.

the insistence of Seventh-day Adventists that we are saved by grace alone — an insistence which distinguishes them, at least in theory, from the Mormons.  But we must add that their acceptance of the doctrine of the investigative judgment, which is not taught in Scripture, has made it impossible for them really to maintain this insistence.  For, in the last analysis, the Adventists teach that it is not the work of Jesus Christ done once for all on the cross, but their faithful keeping of God's commandments and their faithful confession of every single sin that determine whether they are saved or lost.  Sinful deeds committed subsequently to their having accepted Christ may cause God to cancel His forgiveness.  If even the posthumous influence of a person must be taken into account in determining whether he can pass the investigative judgment or not, surely he is not saved by grace alone.

(2) *Teachings on the Sabbath.*  The question of whether Seventh-day Adventists are right in claiming that the seventh day is the proper Lord's Day for us to observe will be treated in Appendix B.  Here we shall examine features of their teachings about the Sabbath Day which support the charge of legalism.  Note first that Seventh-day Adventists virtually elevate the Fourth Commandment above all other commandments.  It will be recalled that Mrs. White reported a vision in which she saw a halo of glory around the Fourth Commandment (above, p. 18).  Mrs. White in her writings pictures the Sabbath as the great test of loyalty, which will divide the inhabitants of the earth into those who obey God and those who submit themselves to earthly powers and consequently receive the mark of the beast.[133]  D. M. Canright reflects upon his own experience as an Adventist when he writes:

> I was long impressed with the fact that we Adventists preached very differently from the apostles.  For instance, we were always preaching and writing about the Sabbath, while Paul in all his fourteen epistles mentions it but once, Col. 2:16, and then only to condemn it![134]

Note further that, according to Seventh-day Adventism, in the latter days all who refuse to keep the seventh day will receive the mark of the beast and be lost.  Though Joseph Bates had taught that all those now keeping the first day as the Sabbath will receive the mark of the beast, the Adventist group has undergone a slight

---

[133] *The Great Controversy*, p. 605.
[134] *Seventh-day Adventism Renounced*, p. 86.

shift in thinking on this point. It is now taught that devout Christians of all faiths who sincerely trust in Christ as Saviour and are following Him according to their best light are saved even though they keep the first day.[135] Just before the return of Christ, however, Sunday observance shall be enforced by law.[136] The world shall then be enlightened concerning the obligation of the true Sabbath.[137] Anyone who shall *then* transgress God's command to keep the seventh day will thereby be honoring Popery above God, and will receive the mark of the beast.[138]

This means, therefore, that in the last days people will not be saved unless they keep the seventh-day Sabbath. At this juncture, certainly, people will be saved at least in part by works. Mere faith in Christ will then not be sufficient.

### DOCTRINE OF THE CHURCH AND SACRAMENTS

#### DOCTRINE OF THE CHURCH

A distinguishing feature of Seventh-day Adventist ecclesiology is that they call themselves the "remnant church." This fact is referred to in next to the last sentence of Article 19 of the *Fundamental Beliefs*: ". . . the gift of the Spirit of prophecy is one of the identifying marks of the remnant church." This fact is also explicitly affirmed in the Seventh-day Adventist *Church Manual*. Among the questions which a candidate for baptism must answer in the affirmative is the following: "Do you believe that the Seventh-day Adventist Church constitutes the remnant church. . .?"[139]

What is meant by the "remnant church"? Revelation 12:17

---

135 *Questions on Doctrine*, p. 184.
136 *Ibid*. It seems hard to imagine such a situation in a world where Sunday is being treated more and more like any other day of the week, particularly by governmental agencies.
137 We are not told by Mrs. White, from whose writings these words are quoted, how this enlightenment shall take place. It seems as though some kind of additional revelation will then be received. The clear implication is that Scripture is not really decisive on this point. If so, why this additional enlightenment?
138 *Ibid*. The material is quoted from Mrs. White's *Great Controversy*, p. 449. The desperate wickedness of people who receive the mark of the beast, therefore, will be that they worship God on Sunday! One sees here to what lengths one may go when he allows an idea to run away with him.
139 *Church Manual*, issued by General Conference of Seventh-day Adventists, 1959; pp. 57-58.

reads as follows in the King James Version: "And the dragon was wroth with the woman, and went to make war with the remnant of her seed, which keep the commandments of God, and have the testimony of Jesus Christ." Seventh-day Adventists say: We are that remnant, or last segment, of the woman's seed of which the Bible here speaks. We are the remnant that keeps the commandments of God because we, in distinction from other Christians, keep the seventh day as the Sabbath. We have the testimony of Jesus Christ: in Revelation 19:10 the testimony of Jesus is defined as "the spirit of prophecy," and we have the Spirit of prophecy in the person of Ellen G. White. We have been raised up by God to proclaim the message of the seventh-day Sabbath shortly before the end of the world in such a way as to declare to all that the keeping of this day is now God's will for His people.[140]

This, of course, brings up immediately the question of whether Seventh-day Adventists believe themselves to be the only true people of God, to the exclusion of all others, including all the major denominations of Christendom. To this question we get an ambiguous answer. On the one hand, the authors of *Questions on Doctrine* assert that they have never sought to equate their church with the church invisible — "those in every denomination who remain faithful to the Scriptures" (p. 186). Seventh-day Adventists, these authors further point out, do not believe that they alone constitute the true children of God (p. 187), that they are the only true Christians in the world, or that they are the only ones who will be saved (pp. 191-92). Elsewhere the authors say: "We fully recognize the heartening fact that a host of true followers of Christ are scattered all through the various churches of Christendom, including the Roman Catholic communion" (p. 197).

On the other hand, however, these authors contend that the Protestant Reformation was incomplete, that God wants certain new truths to be emphasized now which were not proclaimed at the time of the Reformation (p. 189), and that God has given these new truths to the Seventh-day Adventist movement. The heart of this new message is the proclamation of the seventh day

---

[140] *Questions on Doctrine,* pp. 186-96; particularly p. 191. They add, on the last-named page, that this application of the Revelation passage to themselves is the logical conclusion of their system of prophetic interpretation.

as the Sabbath (p. 189). This new message must now be brought to all, even to those orthodox Christians who accept the teachings of the Reformation, for only in this way can Christians prepare for the great test of loyalty which will come in the last days (p. 195).

Do Seventh-day Adventists now really believe that the vast majority of Christians who observe the first day of the week instead of the seventh belong to the universal church of God's true people? Theoretically, they do. We appreciate their willingness to make this statement, which Mormons and Jehovah's Witnesses are unwilling to make. But, once again, we find that their doctrines are not consistent with this statement. For if the seed of the woman spoken of in Revelation 12 is the Christian church, and if the remnant of her seed is the *last segment* of that seed, and if the Seventh-day Adventist Church is that last segment, what conclusion can one arrive at except that other Christian groups are not members of the seed of the woman? If they are, why don't they belong to the remnant?

Furthermore, if the message of the seventh-day Sabbath is now so important that God has raised a special people for its proclamation, and if the keeping of this day is now God's will for all His people, how can men and women who refuse to heed this message still be counted as God's true people? How can Seventh-day Adventists say that there are people "in every denomination who remain faithful to the Scriptures" (p. 186), when these people fail to obey the most important commandment of the Decalogue? How can Adventists contend that these alleged members of the true church outside their fold are "living up to all the light God has given them" (p. 192)? They have the Bible, do they not? Doesn't the Bible give sufficient light on the matter of the seventh day? The authors of *Questions on Doctrine* try to get out of this dilemma by saying, "We respect and love those of our fellow Christians who do not interpret God's Word just as we do" (p. 193). This statement gives the impression that the question of the first day or the seventh is a minor matter on which differences of interpretation may be tolerated. But on another page we are told that Seventh-day Adventists have been raised up by God precisely for the purpose of proclaiming to the world the message of the seventh-day Sabbath! This implies that those Christians who interpret the Word as permitting a first-day Sabbath are dead wrong! How, then, can such utterly mistaken and misguided people be recognized as being faithful to the Scriptures and as belonging to the true church of Jesus Christ?

Since this is a point of great importance, let us look at the matter from another angle. In *Questions on Doctrine* we are told that one who refuses to recognize the deity of Jesus Christ can neither understand nor experience salvation in its fullness. Then follows this statement: "Not only is he disqualified for membership [in the Seventh-day Adventist Church] by his very unbelief, but he is already outside the mystic body of Christ, the church" (p. 45). We take it that by "the mystic body of Christ, the church," the authors mean the invisible church as described above (see p. 129). It is clear, then, from this assertion that one who denies the deity of Christ cannot, according to Seventh-day Adventists, be a member of the invisible church. According to other statements made by these same authors, however, Christians who fail to observe the seventh-day Sabbath can be recognized by Adventists as belonging to the invisible church. Putting these two types of statement together, it would seem that, for Seventh-day Adventists, the observance of the seventh-day Sabbath is far less important than the affirmation of the deity of Jesus Christ. Yet they contend at the same time that God has raised up their movement for the specific purpose of proclaiming to the world the message of the seventh-day Sabbath! The statement in *Questions on Doctrine* (p. 193) about respecting and loving fellow Christians who do not interpret the Bible as the Adventists do, implies that the difference of interpretation about the seventh day is something of such minor importance that it does not hinder one from being included in the invisible church. But if this is so, what reason is there for Seventh-day Adventists to claim that they alone are the remnant church? We conclude that Seventh-day Adventists have no right to claim that they believe that the invisible church is wider than their own fellowship, while at the same time insisting that they are the remnant church of God's most faithful people. They should either repudiate the remnant church concept, or their alleged belief in the invisible church; they cannot with honesty hold on to both.

When Adventists claim that Sunday-keeping Christians can be excused for their transgression of the Fourth Commandment because they are living up to the best light they have, we wonder what they mean. Would deniers of the deity of Christ be excused, since they are living up to the best light they have? If this is not so, as we have seen, why should deniers of the seventh-day Sabbath be excused? The light they live by is the Bible — must this Bible now be damned with faint praise by the expression "the best light they have"? Do Seventh-day Adventists claim to have a *better* light than the Bible? Is this better light, perhaps, provided by the teaching of Mrs. White? And are they now consistent with their alleged dependence on the Bible *alone* as their guide for faith and practice?

We conclude, then, that Seventh-day Adventist teachings on the remnant church are not consistent with their claim that they recognize the existence of an invisible or universal church of Christ which is larger than their fellowship. It should be added that their application of the concept "remnant church" to themselves is neither exegetically nor doctrinally defensible. To begin with the exegetical matter, the idea that Revelation 12:17 refers to a "remnant church" is based on a misinterpretation of the Greek of this passage. The King James Version, to be sure, translates here: "the dragon . . . went to make war with the remnant of her seed." The Greek here, however, does not use either the word *leimma* (translated *remnant* in Rom. 11:5) or the word *hupoleimma* (translated *remnant* in Rom. 9:27, a rendering of the Hebrew *she'ar* in Isa. 10:22), but rather the plural, *hoi loipoi,* literally, "the rest of them." In the American Standard Version, the expression *hoi loipoi* is in every instance translated "the rest." Here, in Revelation 12:17, the expression is rendered in the American Standard: "the rest of her seed"; both the Revised Standard Version and the New English Bible have "the rest of her offspring." The usual interpretation of this passage is that, after having failed to wipe out the church (represented by the woman), Satan (represented by the dragon) now makes war against certain *individual believers*: "the rest of her seed."[141] To read a separate church into this phrase, "the rest of her seed," is completely unwarranted.

Doctrinally the concept of the remnant church is also indefensible. The Scriptures speak about the one body of Christ with its many members (Eph. 4:4-16; I Cor. 12:12-27), and specifically warn against the sin of exalting oneself above other members of

---

[141] This interpretation is found, for example, in R. C. H. Lenski's *Interpretation of St. John's Revelation* (Columbus: Wartburg Press, 1943); W. Hendriksen's *More Than Conquerors* (Grand Rapids: Baker, 1940); and in Albert Barnes's *Notes on the Book of Revelation* (London: Routledge, 1857).

the body of Christ (I Cor. 1:12-13; 3:1-7, 21-23). True, the New Testament does speak of a remnant, in Romans 11:5, "Even so then at this present time also there is a remnant (*leimma*) according to the election of grace." But this is not a remnant *within* the invisible church — this remnant is identical with the invisible church, as far as its Jewish members are concerned. The thought that Seventh-day Adventists are a specific "remnant group" within the invisible or universal church, who are to be distinguished from the rest of the body of Christ as the only really pure and true manifestation of that body, is reminiscent of movements like Montanism, Novatianism, and Donatism, which also claimed to be the true church within the church; and of seventeenth-century pietism, which similarly claimed to be a kind of *ecclesiola in ecclesia* ("a little church within the church"). This is not, however, the Scriptural view of the church. If one wishes to use the term *remnant* at all, as applied to the church, Scriptural usage dictates that the term can only be used to designate the entire invisible church, comprising all true believers, wherever these are found.[142]

### DOCTRINE OF THE SACRAMENTS

*Baptism.* Seventh-day Adventists are opposed to infant baptism, holding that faith, repentance, and acceptance of Christ as Saviour are prerequisites to baptism, and that infants cannot meet these requirements.[143] Article 5 of the *Fundamental Beliefs* specifies that baptism should follow repentance and forgiveness of sins,[144] that by its observance faith is shown in the death, burial, and resurrection of Christ, and that the proper form of baptism is immersion. *Questions on Doctrine* further specifies that this must be a single, not a triple, immersion (p. 23).

The *Church Manual* requires that thorough instruction in the fundamental teachings of the church be given to every candidate for baptism (pp. 46, 48), and that before the person is baptized

---

[142] For additional details on the Seventh-day Adventist view of the remnant church, see *The Four Major Cults*, pp. 396-400.

[143] Branson, *Drama of the Ages*, pp. 167-68.

[144] But how does the church know when a person has truly received the forgiveness of his sins? Can the church read a man's heart? A more accurate expression of this point is found in Article 11 of the Baptismal Vow: ". . . Do you desire to be so baptized as a public expression of your faith in Christ and in the forgiveness of your sins?" (*Church Manual*, p. 57).

there be a public examination, conducted either in the presence
of the church or before the church board (p. 49). The *Manual*
further lists the thirteen questions constituting the Baptismal Vow,
which the candidate must answer in the affirmative (pp. 56-58).

It is expected of the candidate for baptism that he or she shall,
in addition to expressing faith in the Trinity, in Jesus Christ as
Saviour, and in the Bible as God's inspired Word, also assent to
such distinctive Seventh-day Adventist teachings as the seventh-
day Sabbath (Question 6), the Spirit of prophecy (Question 8),
and the remnant church (Question 13). It is also expected that
he will support the church with his tithes and offerings (Question
10) — tithing is thus mandatory for church membership. Of
special interest and significance is Question 7: "Do you believe
that your body is the temple of the Holy Spirit and that you are to
honor God by caring for your body in abstaining from such things
as alcoholic beverages, tobacco in all its forms, and from unclean
foods?"

It is to be observed that Seventh-day Adventists thus make total
abstinence from liquor and tobacco a requirement for church
membership. The *Church Manual,* in fact, lists "among the griev-
ous sins for which members shall be subject to church discipline,"
the following: "the use, manufacture, or sale of alcoholic beverages," and "the use of tobacco or addiction to narcotic drugs"
(pp. 225-26). One wonders by what ethical standards Seventh-
day Adventists can equate the use of tobacco with such sins as
murder, adultery, and stealing (see p. 225). In view of Paul's
words in I Timothy 4:4 ("Every creature of God is good, and
nothing is to be rejected, if it be received with thanksgiving"),
what right does this church have to make total abstinence from
every form of alcoholic beverage a requirement for baptism?

Under the "unclean foods" from which candidates for baptism
must promise to abstain are included such beverages as coffee and
tea, and such meats as pork, ham, shrimp, lobster, and clams. It
will be noted that the meats prohibited are those which the Old
Testament called unclean. Seventh-day Adventists say that they
are well aware of the fact that the ceremonial law which contained
these prohibitions was abolished in New Testament times, but contend that God counseled His people against these articles of diet,
both in Mosaic and pre-Mosaic times, because He knew that they

were not best for human consumption.[145]   Hence, they maintain,
Seventh-day Adventists prohibit these foods for health reasons.

No one can object when a church wishes to improve the health
of its members.   But when one must agree to abstain from certain
foods before he may be baptized, these prohibitions have been
given a religious sanction which takes them out of the category of
mere health measures.   To make abstinence from certain foods a
condition for church membership is adding requirements to those
the Scriptures set before us: true repentance, a living faith in
Jesus Christ, and an earnest resolve to do God's will.   The position
of the Seventh-day Adventist Church on these so-called unclean
foods is condemned not only by I Timothy 4:4-5, the first part
of which was quoted above,[146] but also by Colossians 2:16-17,
"Let no man therefore judge you in meat, or in drink, or in respect of a feast day or a new moon or a sabbath day:  which are
a shadow of the things to come; but the body is Christ's."[147]

*The Lord's Supper.* It seems strange that no mention is made of
the Lord's Supper in the *Fundamental Beliefs.* According to the
*Church Manual,* however, Seventh-day Adventists are to observe
the Lord's Supper once every three months (p. 111).   This service
is announced on the preceding week, at which time the members of
the congregation are urged to prepare their hearts and to make
sure that matters are right with one another (p. 111).   An unusual
feature of their Lord's Supper celebration is that it is always pre-
ceded by the ordinance of footwashing.   Mrs. White taught that,
when Jesus washed the disciples' feet prior to His institution of the
Lord's Supper, He was not simply teaching the disciples a lesson in
humility; He was instituting a religious ceremony (p. 115).[148] Branson, in fact, maintains that this ordinance symbolizes the "lesser
cleansing" in distinction from baptism, which is the "greater cleansing" — footwashing thus pictures the forgiveness of sins which
have accumulated since baptism.[149]   The *Manual* further states

---

[145] *Questions on Doctrine,* p. 623.

[146] Note particularly the preceding context, where "commanding to
abstain from meats" (v. 3) is listed as a "doctrine of demons" (v. 1).

[147] See F. F. Bruce's excellent comment on these verses in his *Commentary on Colossians* (Eerdmans, 1957).   For a good treatment
of the whole question of "unclean foods" in Seventh-day Adventism, see
Chapter 7 of Bird's *Theology of Seventh-day Adventism.*

[148] Quoted from *The Desire of Ages,* p. 650.

[149] *Op. cit.,* pp. 183-84.   Note that Branson's explanation here implies
that Seventh-day Adventists are not perfectionists.

that the men and women are separated for this ordinance, each member washing the feet of the person next to him (pp. 111-12).[150]

The *Manual* calls the Lord's Supper itself a memorial of the crucifixion of Christ (p. 114). Yet it is more than a mere sign; it also strengthens faith: "participation [in the Lord's Supper] by members of the body is essential to Christian growth and fellowship" (p. 55). The *Church Manual* further specifies that every member shall attend the Lord's Supper (p. 114); when people who are visiting the church wish to take part in the service, they shall not be forbidden (p. 113). Seventh-day Adventists use unleavened bread and unfermented wine in the Lord's Supper (p. 114). Any bread or wine which is left over after the service is to be disposed of as follows: the bread is to be burned and the wine is to be poured out (p. 116).

## DOCTRINE OF THE LAST THINGS

### INDIVIDUAL ESCHATOLOGY

*The State of Man after Death.*   When we examined the Seventh-day Adventist doctrine of man, we learned that Adventists do not believe that man, either as a whole or in part, is inherently immortal, or that man has a soul which can survive the death of the body. We noted also that they interpret the Biblical word *soul* (*nephesh* or *psuchee*) as meaning the entire individual rather than an immaterial aspect of man, and that it is therefore better to say that a person *is* a soul than that he *has* a soul.[151]

What, now, does this position imply as to the state of man after death? We find the answer in Article 10 of the *Fundamental Beliefs*: "That the condition of man in death is one of unconsciousness. That all men, good and evil alike, remain in the grave from death to the resurrection." Here is the way one Seventh-day Adventist author explains their position on this matter:

> The teaching of the Bible regarding the intermediate state of man is plain. Death is really and truly a sleep, a sleep that is deep, that is unconscious, that is unbroken until the awakening at the resurrection.
>
> In death man enters a state of sleep. The language of the Bible makes clear that it is the whole man which sleeps, not

---

150 Cf. Branson, *op. cit.*, p. 185.
151 See above, pp. 33-34.

merely a part. No intimation is given that man sleeps only as to his body, and that he is wakeful and conscious as to his soul. All that comprises the man sleeps in death.[152]

Note that, according to Mr. Haynes, it is not the soul that sleeps, but man. The same position is taken by the authors of *Questions on Doctrine* (pp. 511-32). It is therefore not quite accurate to say, as some do, that the Seventh-day Adventists teach the doctrine of *soul-sleep*, since this would imply that there is a soul which continues to exist after death, but in an unconscious state. A more precise way of characterizing their teachings on this point is to say that the Adventists teach *soul-extinction*. For, according to them, *soul* is simply another name for the entire individual; there is, therefore, no soul that survives after death. After death nothing survives; when man dies he becomes completely nonexistent.

Seventh-day Adventists do teach that there will be a resurrection of all men. The authors of *Questions on Doctrine* state that the time interval between death and the resurrection is negligible, since there is no consciousness in the so-called "intermediate state":

> While asleep in the tomb the child of God knows nothing. Time matters not to him. If he should be there a thousand years, the time would be to him as but a moment. One who serves God closes his eyes in death, and whether one day or two thousand years elapse, the next instant in his consciousness will be when he opens his eyes and beholds his blessed Lord. To him it is death — then sudden glory (pp. 523-24).

*Conditional Immortality.* Article 9 of the *Fundamental Beliefs* sets forth the Adventist position on immortality:

> That "God only hath immortality" (I Tim. 6:16). Mortal man possesses a nature inherently sinful and dying. Eternal life is the gift of God through faith in Christ (Rom. 6:23). . . . Immortality is bestowed upon the righteous at the Second Coming of Christ, when the righteous dead are raised from the grave and the living righteous translated to meet the Lord. Then it is that those accounted faithful "put on immortality" (I Cor. 15:51-55).

Seventh-day Adventists thus believe in *conditional immortality*: immortality is bestowed upon believers at the Second Coming of Christ. Man possesses no inherent immortality, and man has no immortal soul. Immortality in the absolute sense is possessed only

---

152 Carlyle B. Haynes, *Life, Death, and Immortality*, p. 202.

by God. Immortality in a relative sense is bestowed only upon certain people — namely, those who believe. Unbelievers will be raised from the dead after the millennium, but they will not receive immortality. They will be raised only to be annihilated.[153]

## GENERAL ESCHATOLOGY

*The Return of Christ.* As their denominational name indicates, the Second Coming of Christ is one of the cardinal doctrines of the Adventist faith. Seventh-day Adventists believe in the literal, physical, audible, visible, and personal return of Christ.[154] They look upon this Second Coming as "the great hope of the church, the grand climax of the gospel and plan of salvation."[155] Whereas Seventh-day Adventism owes its origin to the attempt by William Miller to set the date for Christ's return, present-day Adventists no longer try to set such a date. In *Questions on Doctrine* they now affirm: ". . . We believe that our Lord's return is imminent, at a time that is near but not disclosed" (p. 463).

It is clearly affirmed that the Return of Christ will be a single coming, not a two-stage advent. Seventh-day Adventists therefore differ from dispensational premillennialists in rejecting a pretribulational secret rapture — that is, in rejecting the doctrine that the church will be secretly and silently snatched from the earth before the Great Tribulation (p. 454). Though they agree with premillennialists that there will be a millennium, they deny that this millennium will be marked by an earthly reign of Christ over the converted Jewish nation; they therefore see no particular prophetic significance in the establishment of the modern state of Israel in Palestine (pp. 234-35). In fact, they indicate ten respects in which they differ from dispensational premillennialism (pp. 239-40).

*The Battle of Armageddon.* The final conflict among the nations will be the Battle of Armageddon. Taking their cue from Revelation 16:12-16, Seventh-day Adventists contend that the history of this world will be brought to an end in this great battle, called in Scripture "the battle of that great day of God Al-

---

[153] Jehovah's Witnesses take virtually the same position on the intermediate state as do Seventh-day Adventists. Note that acceptance of the doctrine of conditional immortality implies a denial of eternal punishment. In Appendix E of *The Four Major Cults* these doctrines (soul-extinction, conditional immortality, and the annihilation of the wicked) are critically evaluated.

[154] *Questions on Doctrine*, pp. 449-54, 463.

[155] *Fundamental Beliefs*, Article 20.

mighty."[156]  The warfare between nations which has always marked man's history will culminate in this great battle, which will be fought in the plain of Megiddo in central Palestine.  This will not, however, be simply a war between nations: "At Armageddon international, inter-racial, and inter-religious strife will give place to that phase of man's effort to retain the dominion of this earth described in Rev. 19:19, as a contest between the armies of earth and the armies of heaven."[157]  Since the three symbolic characters mentioned in Revelation 16:13 (the dragon, the beast, and the false prophet) represent the false religious systems of the world, both heathen and professed Christian, the Battle of Armageddon will be a "holy war" between God and His people on the one side, and the devil and his people (apostate Christians as well as the devotees of false religions) on the other side.[158]

This war will be interrupted and brought to a sudden end by the personal and visible return of Jesus Christ.[159]  Christ will now break the nations with a rod of iron and "dash them in pieces like a potter's vessel," thus utterly defeating His enemies.[160]  At this time the day of salvation will be past.[161]  The beast and the false prophet are now cast alive into the lake of fire.  All the unrighteous who have not by this time been killed in battle are now put to death, being "destroyed by the brightness of Christ's visible presence."[162]

*The Binding of Satan.*  The binding of Satan spoken of in Revelation 20:1-3 now occurs.  This is interpreted to mean that Satan is consigned by divine command to the desolate earth, which is understood to be the "abyss" or "bottomless pit" of Revelation 20:3.  As we have seen, the wicked or unrighteous have by this time all been put to death.  This has left only believers on the earth.  They, however, as we shall see in a moment, are about to

---

[156] Branson, *op. cit.*, p. 525.  Cf. Carlyle B. Haynes, *The Return of Jesus* (Washington: Review and Herald, 1926), p. 279.

[157] Haynes, *Return of Jesus*, p. 287.

[158] Branson, *op. cit.*, pp. 531-33.

[159] Haynes, *Return of Jesus*, p. 287.

[160] *Ibid.*, pp. 287, 295.

[161] Branson, *op. cit.*, p. 536.  Note that Seventh-day Adventists do not teach the possibility of a second chance to be saved after one has died, or after this point in history has been reached.  On this point see *ibid.*, p. 211.

[162] *Questions on Doctrine*, pp. 491-92.  From p. 495 we learn that Christ at this time does not actually come all the way down to the earth, but remains in the air.

be translated to heaven. Thus, during the millennium which is
about to begin, the earth will be completely desolate of human
habitation. To this desolate earth Satan, with his fallen-angel
companions, will be confined for a thousand years. This will give
him ample time to ponder on the results of his rebellion against
God.[163]

This teaching must be seen in connection with Seventh-day Adventist doctrine about Satan as the one upon whom the sins of
the world will be laid. As we have seen, the Adventists see a par-
allel between what happened to the second goat on the Day of
Atonement and what will be done to Satan after Christ returns.
Just as the so-called scapegoat was sent away into an uninhabited
wilderness after the sins of the people had been confessed over his
head, so Satan, after the sins of the world have been placed upon
him, will be banished to the desolate earth, which during the millennium will be a dreary, uninhabited wilderness.[164]

*The Special Resurrection.* Seventh-day Adventists believe in
three resurrections, one special and two general. The two general resurrections are those of believers and unbelievers, respec-
tively, the former occurring at the beginning of the millennium,
the latter at the end of the millennium. Before discussing these,
however, we must take note of the special resurrection, which will
occur before either of the two general resurrections. It will take
place just before the Second Coming of Christ, and will involve
some unbelievers and some believers. We therefore interrupt the
chronological sequence briefly at this point in order to describe
this special resurrection.

The first of the two groups to be raised at this time consists of
those who were responsible for the trial and crucifixion of Christ.
Basing her comment on Revelation 1:7, Mrs. White says,

> "They also which pierced Him" (Rev. 1:7), those that mocked
> and derided Christ's dying agonies, and the most violent opposers
> of His truth and His people, are raised to behold Him in His
> glory, and to see the honor placed upon the loyal and obedient.[165]

---

[163] *Ibid.*, p. 492. Cf. also Branson, *op. cit.*, pp. 551-54; and Haynes, *The Return of Jesus*, pp. 295-303.

[164] *Questions on Doctrine*, pp. 498-501; see also Ellen G. White, *The Great Controversy*, p. 658

[165] *The Great Controversy*, p. 637. Since all the unrighteous who are not killed in the Battle of Armageddon will be destroyed by the brightness of Christ's presence, and since all the wicked will be raised at the end

The second of these two groups consists of those who "died in
the faith of the third angel's message." In a personal letter (June
4, 1963) sent to the author by Mr. Thomas H. Blincoe of Andrews
University at Berrien Springs, Michigan (the Seventh-day Adventist Theological Seminary), the following statement was made:

> In Revelation 14:13, just at the close of the third angel's
> message of Revelation 14:9-12, there appears this beatitude:
> "Blessed are the dead which die in the Lord from henceforth."
> We believe that all those who die in the Lord "in the faith of
> the third angel's message" will be granted a singular blessing
> in the form of being raised in the special resurrection before
> the glorious return of Christ and will thus have the privilege
> of seeing Him come. The third angel's message began to be
> preached about 1846.

The above statement is based on the following words from Mrs.
White:

> Graves are open, and "many of them that sleep in the dust of
> the earth . . . awake, some to everlasting life, and some to shame
> and everlasting contempt" (Dan. 12:2). All who have died in
> the faith of the third angel's message come forth from the tomb
> glorified, to hear God's covenant of peace with those who have
> kept His law.[166]

As we saw earlier,[167] the third angel's message of Revelation
14 is interpreted by Seventh-day Adventists as requiring the observance of the seventh day. Those who have "died in the faith of
the third angel's message," therefore, must be the faithful members
of the Seventh-day Adventist denomination who have passed
away since 1846 (and any others who have been heeding this
message since that time). It appears, then, that loyal and obedi-
ent Seventh-day Adventists will be granted a special, pre-Second-
Advent resurrection, so that they may have the privilege of seeing
Christ's return.

*The Resurrection and Transformation of Believers.* After
Christ has returned and after Satan has been bound, there occurs
the general resurrection of believers. Seventh-day Adventists fol-

---

of the millennium, it would appear that the individuals brought to life
in this phase of the special resurrection will be raised twice: once now, and
once at the end of the millennium.

[166] *Ibid.*, It is made clear that both groups just described will be raised
before Christ's actual return. See on this point also *Principles of Life
from the Word of God*, pp. 327-28, 480-81.

[167] See above, p. 16.

low the Revised Standard Version in translating Revelation 20:4 as follows: "they [the souls of those who had been beheaded] came to life again, and reigned with Christ a thousand years."[168] At this point, therefore, all true believers who died before 1846, and all who died in the Lord since 1846 but who "never heard and came under the conviction of the truth revealed by the third angel's message,"[169] will be raised.  It will be remembered, however, that this is not strictly a resurrection, since there are no souls of these believers which are still in existence.  Actually, since no aspect of these believers is still in existence, and since therefore these individuals have been completely annihilated, it would seem to be more accurate to call their restoration to life a *new creation* rather than a resurrection.  God, it may be presumed, now creates them anew on the basis of His memory of what they were like before they died.[170]

After this resurrection, all believers who are still alive (and only believers are left alive at this point) will be transformed and glorified.  Now both the resurrected believers and the transformed believers will be caught up in the clouds to meet Christ in the air; after this they are taken up by Him to heaven.[171]

*The Millennium.*  At this point the millennium begins, during which the saints will reign with Christ in heaven for a thousand years.  On this point Seventh-day Adventists distinguish themselves from premillennialists, who picture the millennium as involving an earthly reign by Christ in Palestine over a kingdom consisting chiefly of converted Jews.  For the Adventists, the millennial reign is neither earthly nor Jewish, but heavenly.[172]

During this millennial period the saints engage in a work of judgment.  This thought is derived from Revelation 20:4, "And I saw thrones, and they sat upon them, and judgment was given unto them."  The question now arises:  what is the nature of this judgment?  The investigative judgment has been completed as far as believers are concerned.  As far as unbelievers are concerned, decisions regarding their punishment have not yet been

---

[168] *Questions on Doctrine,* p. 493.  It should be observed, however, that the Greek word used here, *ezeesan,* can also be rendered simply *they lived,* and is so rendered both by the King James and American Standard Versions.
[169] Letter from Thomas Blincoe referred to above.
[170] *Questions on Doctrine,* pp. 493-94.
[171] *Ibid.,* pp. 494-96.
[172] *Ibid.,* pp. 479-80, 495.

finally arrived at. Seventh-day Adventists teach that during the millennium the saints engage, together with Christ, in a work of judgment, a work which involves "a careful investigation of the records of evil men and a decision regarding the amount of punishment due each sinner for his part in the rebellion against God."[173]

One wonders how there can be variations in the amount of punishment meted out to the wicked when, according to Seventh-day Adventist teaching, all the wicked will be annihilated. Their answer is that this variation will be evident in the amount of suffering which will precede the annihilation of the wicked.[174]

*The Resurrection of the Wicked.* In the King James Version Revelation 20:5a reads as follows: "The rest of the dead lived not again until the thousand years were finished." Seventh-day Adventists interpret this verse to mean that the wicked will be raised at the end of the millennium. At this time Christ, accompanied by all the saints, will descend to earth again — only now He will not remain in the air, but will come all the way down to earth. He will now command all the wicked dead to arise. In answer to this summons all the unbelieving dead are brought back to life, and begin to spread over the earth, having the same rebellious spirit which possessed them in life.[175]

*Satan Loosed.* Through the resurrection of the wicked, Satan is loosed for a "little season" (Rev. 20:3). His enforced idleness now over, he sees the innumerable host of resurrected unbelievers, and determines to make one last attempt to overthrow God's kingdom. Deceiving the risen wicked into thinking that they can take the city of God by force, Satan gathers his hosts into battle array for a final, futile assault upon the "camp of the saints" — the new Jerusalem which has just descended with Christ from heaven. In this great battle the entire human race meets face to face, for the first and the last time.[176]

*Satan, the Demons, and the Wicked Annihilated.* This great battle — not to be confused with the Battle of Armageddon at the beginning of the millennium — ends in Satan's final defeat. Fire

---

[173] *Ibid.*, pp. 496-98.
[174] *Ibid.*, p. 498.
[175] *Ibid.*, p. 504. The retention of this rebellious spirit is difficult to understand in view of the fact that, according to Adventist teaching, their death meant their complete annihilation, and their so-called resurrection is really a new creation.
[176] *Ibid.*, p. 505.

comes down from God out of heaven and annihilates Satan, his evil angels, and all the wicked. This annihilation Seventh-day Adventists call the second death; before the annihilation, however, there will be gradations of suffering, depending upon the guilt of the person or demon involved. Since Satan is the most guilty of all God's creatures, he will suffer the longest and will therefore be the last to perish in the flames.[177] At the end of this period of suffering, however, all those who have rebelled against God will have been wiped out of existence:

> . . . The finally impenitent, including Satan, the author of sin, will, by the fires of the last day, be reduced to a state of nonexistence, becoming as though they had not been, thus purging God's universe of sin and sinners.[178]

Seventh-day Adventists thus reject the doctrine of hell as it has always been taught by historic Christianity. They do claim, however, to believe in eternal punishment; annihilation, they say, can be called eternal punishment because it is eternal in its results.[179]

---

[177] *Ibid.,* pp. 498, 534; Branson, *op. cit.,* p. 567.

[178] *Fundamental Beliefs,* Article 12. If this is so, one wonders why God went to all the trouble of "raising" the wicked. Would it not have been simpler just to leave them in the state of nonexistence to which their physical death had reduced them?

[179] *Questions on Doctrine,* p. 539. A critical evaluation of these teachings on future punishment can be found in Appendix E of *The Four Major Cults.* See the competent refutation of these doctrines in Norman Douty, *op. cit.,* pp. 142-159, and in Bird, *op. cit.,* pp. 53-63.

At this point it should be noted that Seventh-day Adventists differ from historic Christianity in denying the doctrine of the public Day of Judgment. The great Protestant creeds affirm that there will be a Day of Judgment after Christ returns to earth, and after the resurrection of both believers and unbelievers has taken place. All persons who have ever lived shall then appear before the judgment-seat of Christ, to be publicly judged on the basis of their personal relationship to Christ during this life, and on the basis of their works (see Augsburg Confession, Part I, Art. 17; Belgic Confession, Art. 37; Westminster Confession, Chap. 33 — or 35, in more recent editions).

Seventh-day Adventists, however, deny that there shall be a public judgment of the sort described above. The judgment referred to in Rev. 20:12 they understand as meaning the investigative judgment which is going on now (*Questions on Doctrine,* p. 421). They distinguish, however, between *investigative judgments* and *executive judgments* (p. 422). There are, according to them, two phases in the process of judgment: the *investigative judgment* of believers, which is going on now, which will be completed before Christ's Second Coming, and which will be followed by the *executive judgment* of believers that will occur at the Second Coming; and the *investigative judgment* of unbelievers, which will be carried on during the millennium, and which will be followed by the *executive judgment* of unbelievers, to take place after the millennium.

*The New Earth.* "In the conflagration which destroys Satan and his hosts, the earth itself will be regenerated and cleansed from the effects of the curse."[180] So out of the ruins of the old earth there will spring forth a new earth, which the redeemed will occupy as their everlasting home.

> . . . God will make all things new. The earth, restored to its pristine beauty, will become forever the abode of the saints of the Lord. The promise to Abraham, that through Christ he and his seed should possess the earth throughout the endless ages of eternity, will be fulfilled.[181]

On this new earth Christ will reign supreme, and all the saints shall forever serve, obey, and glorify Him.[182]

---

In each case the executive judgment is simply the execution of the sentence of judgment which has been determined by the investigative judgment.
[180] *Fundamental Beliefs,* Article 21.
[181] *Ibid.,* Article 22.
[182] *Ibid.* Cf. *Questions on Doctrine,* pp. 507-8; and Branson, *op. cit.,* pp. 573-82. For additional details on Seventh-day Adventist eschatology, see *The Four Major Cults,* pp. 400-403.

# IV. Appendix A: The Investigative Judgment and the Scapegoat Doctrine in Seventh-day Adventism

## THE INVESTIGATIVE JUDGMENT

Having previously set forth what Seventh-day Adventists teach about the investigative judgment and about Satan as the antitype of the Old Testament scapegoat, I should like in this appendix to subject these doctrines to a Scriptural evaluation. The very first thing we should remember about these teachings is that they arose as the result of a mistake. It was William Miller's erroneous interpretation of Daniel 8:14, it will be recalled, which was the occasion for the formation of these theological constructions. Miller understood the "cleansing of the sanctuary" of Daniel 8:14 to mean Christ's return to earth; he further understood the 2300 evenings and mornings mentioned in this passage as standing for 2300 years; and, using the year 457 B.C. as the starting date for the 2300 years, he predicted that Christ would return from heaven some time between March 21, 1843, and March 21, 1844. Later Miller, following the leadership of Samuel Snow, moved the date ahead to October 22, 1844.[1]

When Christ did not return to earth on this date, Miller himself was convinced that he had been mistaken. On the following morning, however, Hiram Edson had a vision of Christ entering the holy of holies of the heavenly sanctuary. On the basis of

[1] See above, pp. 9-12.

this vision he now began to reinterpret Miller's prediction as having had reference not to Christ's return to earth, but to Christ's entrance into the second apartment of the heavenly sanctuary in order to cleanse it. This reinterpretation was adopted by Adventist leaders and became the basis for Seventh-day Adventist teachings on the investigative judgment and on Satan as the antitype of the scapegoat.[2] Mrs. White had a vision confirming this reinterpretation in February of 1845, and Mr. Crosier expanded this reinterpretation into an article in an Adventist periodical in February of 1846 — and thus the doctrine was firmly entrenched as an irrevocable part of Seventh-day Adventist theology.

No Bible expositor, however, had ever found this teaching in the Bible previous to this time. No individual or group outside the Seventh-day Adventists has ever taught it since that time. As we shall see, there is no Biblical basis for this doctrine. The conclusion is inescapable that Seventh-day Adventist teaching on the investigative judgment was simply a way out of an embarrassing predicament. Instead of admitting, as Miller himself did, that a very serious error had been made in Scripture interpretation, these Adventist leaders clung frantically to the date Miller had set, and gave to that date a meaning which he himself never acknowledged. The doctrine of the investigative judgment, therefore, one of the key doctrines of Seventh-day Adventism, was a doctrine built on a mistake!

Closer scrutiny of the eighth chapter of Daniel's prophecy will reveal that verse 14 says nothing about either the return of Christ from heaven or His entrance into the holy of holies of the heavenly sanctuary. The chapter itself indicates that the two-horned ram which Daniel saw in his vision (v. 3) stood for the kings of Media and Persia (v. 20). The he-goat (v. 5) is interpreted by the angel as standing for the king of Greece (v. 21). Obviously, then, the casting down of the ram by the he-goat (v. 7) stands for the defeat of the Medo-Persian empire by Greece. It is presumed by most interpreters that the coming up of four horns on the head of the he-goat instead of the one great horn (v. 8) stands for the division of Alexander the Great's empire into four kingdoms after the latter's death (see v. 22).

What, now, is to be understood by the "little horn, which

[2] See above, pp. 12-15.

waxed exceeding great, toward the south, and toward the east, and toward the glorious land" (v. 9)? Verse 23 gives us the answer: this little horn stands for a person, "a king of fierce countenance." In the light of what verses 11 and 12 tell us, we may be reasonably sure that this person was Antiochus Epiphanes, ruler of Syria from 175-164 B.C., who did cast down the Jewish sanctuary (v. 11) by profaning it, and who did take away the continual burnt offering (v. 11) by stopping all Jewish sacrifices in the temple and substituting pagan sacrifices for them. Daniel now hears one holy one asking another, "How long shall be the vision concerning the continual burnt-offering, and the transgression that maketh desolate, to give both the sanctuary and the host to be trodden underfoot?"[3]

The answer to this question is given in verse 14: "And he said unto me, Unto two thousand and three hundred evenings and mornings; then shall the sanctuary be cleansed" (ASV). It has been noted previously that the Hebrew word translated *cleansed* is actually the Niphal form of the verb *tsadaq,* which in the Qal means *to be right or righteous*; in the Niphal the verb therefore means *to be put right.*[4] It is unfortunate that the word came to be translated *be cleansed,* since the Hebrew verb usually rendered cleansed is not used here at all.[5] The Brown-Driver-Briggs Hebrew lexicon suggests that this part of the verse be translated: "the holy place shall be put right" (p. 842); the RSV, as previously observed, renders: "then the sanctuary shall be restored to its rightful state." The thought of this verse is not cleansing from sin, but restoration to its right and proper condition or use.

The part of verse 14 which gives the length of time designated reads literally as follows: "Until evening morning two thousand

---

[3] Verse 13, in the ASV. The expression "to be trodden underfoot" is a translation of a Hebrew noun, *mirmas,* and means literally, "for trampling." The reader's attention is called to this word, since it is obvious that the sanctuary here spoken of is not a heavenly one. A heavenly sanctuary cannot be trampled underfoot.

[4] See above, p. 11, n. 6.

[5] *Taheer* in the Pi'el. It is significant that it is this verb which is used in Lev. 16 — the chapter which describes the ceremonies of the Day of Atonement. It is used once (v. 19) of the cleansing of the altar which is before Jehovah (probably the altar of burnt-offering), and once (v. 30) of the cleansing of the people from their sins. Certainly if Daniel meant to refer to the kind of cleansing which was done on the Day of Atonement, he would have used *taheer* instead of *tsadaq.*

and three hundreds." The words for evening and morning are in the singular, and there is no connective between them. The previous reference to the continual burnt offering — offered every morning and every evening — implies that these words in verse 14 have reference to these two daily sacrifices. The fact that these offerings had been stopped, and that the question was asked, "How long?" implies that the answer will be in terms of the number of these daily burnt offerings. Thus the obvious and natural interpretation of the words "until evening morning two thousand and three hundreds" is: until 2300 morning and evening burnt offerings. Since two of these occurred every day, this means 1150 days.

This number of days, according to Jewish reckoning, would be equivalent to three years and some 50 or 60 days. By comparing I Maccabees 1:54 and 59 with 4:52-53, we learn that a period of exactly three years elapsed between the offering of the first heathen sacrifice upon the altar of burnt offering in the temple court and the resumption of regular sacrifices on this altar after the temple had been won back from Antiochus Epiphanes by Judas Maccabeus (from Dec. 25, 168 B.C. to Dec. 25, 165 B.C.). However, the order to stop offering the regular morning and evening sacrifices on this altar had been given some time prior to Dec. 25, 168 B.C.; thus we can account for the additional 50 or 60 days.[6] In the light of what was said above about the meaning of the verb here used, does it not seem natural and obvious that Daniel 8:14 predicts the restoration of the earthly sanctuary to its rightful and proper use after a period of desecration by a heathen king? The 2300 evenings and mornings, then, picture the period of a little more than three years during which this desecration occurred, and the "putting right" of the sanctuary refers to the end of this period of desecration, on the 25th day of December, 165 B.C.[7]

[6] G. Ch. Aalders, *Het Boek Daniel* (in *Korte Verklaring* series; 2nd printing; Kampen: Kok, 1951), pp. 178-79.

[7] This interpretation of Daniel 8:14 is the one advanced by Aalders, the late Professor of Old Testament at the Free University in Amsterdam, in the volume mentioned above. See also J. K. Van Baalen, *Chaos of Cults* (4th ed.; Grand Rapids: Eerdmans, 1962), p. 233, n. 9. C. F. Keil, in his *Commentary on Daniel* (Edinburgh: Clark, 1891) and Edward J. Young in his *Prophecy of Daniel* (Grand Rapids: Eerdmans, 1953) are both of the opinion that the 2300 evenings and mornings must be interpreted, not as 1150 days, but as 2300 days. Yet both understand the "cleansing" or "putting right" of the sanctuary as referring to its restoration to proper use after its desecration by Antiochus Epiphanes. Both there-

The doctrine of the investigative judgment, as taught by Seventh-day Adventists, ought therefore to be rejected by all Christians, and by the Adventists themselves, as unscriptural and untrue. For this assertion I advance the following reasons:

(1) The doctrine of the investigative judgment *is based on a mistaken interpretation of Daniel 8:14.* It has been shown above that when Seventh-day Adventists find in Daniel 8:14 a prediction of a cleansing of the heavenly sanctuary by Christ, which cleansing was to begin on October 22, 1844, they are reading something into this passage which simply is not there.

(2) This doctrine *is based on a mistaken understanding of the Old Testament sacrificial system.* This misunderstanding reveals itself, first, in the supposition that the sprinkling of the blood of the daily or occasional sacrifices by the Old Testament priests polluted the sanctuary, whereas the sprinkling of the blood of the goat slain on the Day of Atonement cleansed the sanctuary. We have noted above that Crosier advanced this conception in his *Day-Star* article, and that L. E. Froom, in his own elaboration of Crosier's ideas, likewise accepted it (above, pp. 13-14). We find this same conception in *Questions on Doctrine* (pp. 431-32). Why, however, should the sprinkling of sacrificial blood in one instance pollute the sanctuary, and in the other instance cleanse it? Why should such sprinkling of blood mean, in one instance, that the sin involved was now recorded in the sanctuary, and, in the other instance, that the sin was removed from the sanctuary?

We may press this point a bit further. If the blood of sin offerings, for instance, when sprinkled upon the altar of burnt offering, served to transfer the offerer's guilt to the altar and thus to pollute the altar, why should not the blood of the slain goat on the Day of Atonement, when sprinkled upon the mercy seat, serve to transfer the guilt of the people to the mercy seat and thus to pollute the mercy seat? On the other hand, if the blood sprinkled upon the mercy seat served to remove guilt, why should not blood sprinkled upon the altar of burnt offering at the time of every ordinary sin-offering serve to remove guilt?

When Seventh-day Adventists say, "When the blood was sprinkled, the sin was recorded in the sanctuary," adding that it was only on the Day of Atonement that the accumulated record

---

fore agree basically with the interpretation advanced above (though differing on the time period involved), and disavow the Seventh-day Adventist interpretation of this passage.

of the sins of the year was removed from the sanctuary,[8] we must reply that they have completely failed to grasp the significance of the sprinkling of the sacrificial blood upon the altar. The Bible itself makes quite clear what the significance of this sprinkling was. After warning the people against eating blood, the Lord through Moses gave the reason for this prohibition: "For the life (*nephesh*) of the flesh is in the blood; and I have given it to you upon the altar to make atonement (*kapper*) for your souls (*naphshootheekhem*); for it is the blood that maketh atonement (*yekappeer*) by reason of the life (*nephesh*)" (Lev. 17:11). The verb *kipper* in the Pi'el means to cover over, or to make propitiation. The verse just quoted states clearly that the blood upon the altar made propitiation for the souls of the offerers; there is no indication whatever that this happened only on the Day of Atonement. If this blood when applied to the altar made propitiation for the offerer and covered his sin, on what ground can Adventists claim that the application of blood to the altar meant that the sin of the offerer was now recorded in the sanctuary?

Note how Patrick Fairbairn, whose two-volume *Typology of Scripture* is one of the classic works on this subject, explains the symbolism of the sprinkling of blood upon the altar:

> Having with his own hands executed the deserved penalty on the victim, the offerer gave the blood to the priest, as God's representative. But that blood had already paid, in death, the penalty of sin, and was no longer laden with guilt and pollution. The justice of God was (symbolically) satisfied concerning it; and by the hands of His own representative He could with perfect consistence receive it as a pure and spotless thing, the very image of His own holiness, upon His table or altar. In being received there, however, it still represented the blood or soul of the offerer, who thus saw himself, through the action with the blood of his victim, re-established in communion with God, and solemnly recognized as received back to the divine favor and fellowship.[9]

[8] *Questions on Doctrine,* p. 432.
[9] II, 275. The quotation is from the 10th ed. (New York: Tibbals, n.d.). Cf. Louis Berkhof, *Biblical Archaeology* (3rd ed.; Grand Rapids: Smitter, 1928), p. 146; and G. F. Oehler, *Theology of the Old Testament,* trans. George E. Day (New York: Funk & Wagnalls, 1883), pp. 276-281. The last author adds the thought that the sprinkling of the blood represents symbolically the self-surrender of the offerer to God. See also J. D. Douglas, ed., *The New Bible Dictionary* (Grand Rapids: Eerdmans, 1962), pp. 1120-22.

One might still ask, however: If the daily sacrifices served to propitiate for sin so that no record of these sins was left in the sanctuary, why was a Day of Atonement necessary? What Seventh-day Adventists teach on this point will be evident from the following quotation:

> On the Day of Atonement, when the blood of the goat was sprinkled upon all the furniture of the sanctuary as well as upon the altar of burnt offering, the accumulated record of the sins of the year were [should be: was] removed. . . . The sins of the Israelites, recorded in the sanctuary by the shed blood of the sacrificial victims, were removed and totally disposed of on the Day of Atonement.[10]

In reply, it may be pointed out that, according to Leviticus 16:33, the high priest on the Day of Atonement had to make atonement (*kipper*) for the holy sanctuary, the tent of meeting, the altar (of burnt offering), the priests, and "all the people of the assembly." If, now, as Seventh-day Adventists claim, the purpose of these ceremonies was to remove accumulated sins which had been recorded, they would have to grant that these accumulated sins had been recorded upon the people as well as in the sanctuary. But the whole thrust of their argumentation is that by the daily sacrifices the guilt of these sins was taken from the people and transferred to the sanctuary.[11] It should also be noted that both in verse 16 and verse 33 of this chapter the Hebrew word used to describe the atonement that was made for the sanctuary on the Day of Atonement is *kipper*. In this chapter, according to the Adventists, *kipper* means the complete removal of sins from the sanctuary. But why, then, does the word not have the same meaning in Leviticus 17:11, quoted above, where it refers to every application of blood upon the altar?

If, however, the daily sacrifices did serve to propitiate for sin (on the basis, of course, of the sacrifice of Christ which was to come), why were the ceremonies of the Day of Atonement necessary? To this question a twofold answer may be given: (i) This general expiation for sin would serve to cover those sins, both of the people and of the priests, for which offerings had

---

[10] *Questions on Doctrine*, p. 432.
[11] "The individual sinner was forgiven and thus freed from his sin, but in the bloodstains of the sanctuary he could perceive in type a record of the misdeeds that he would fain see blotted out and removed forever" (*Questions on Doctrine*, p. 432).

not been made during the previous year;[12] and (ii) the entrance of the high priest into the holy of holies was a prediction of the future removal of the evil which separated the people from God, and an anticipation of the work of our great High Priest, Jesus Christ, who was to enter in "once for all into the holy place, having obtained eternal redemption" (Heb. 9:12).[13] We conclude, therefore, that the contention of Seventh-day Adventists, that the daily offerings served to transfer sins to the sanctuary, and that the sacrifices of the Day of Atonement served to remove these sins and thus to cleanse the sanctuary, is not in harmony with the facts. Since this contention is basic to their construction of the investigative judgment, we observe at this point that one of the pillars on which this doctrine rests has been overthrown.

A second misunderstanding of the Old Testament sacrificial system found among Seventh-day Adventists is the view that the morning and evening sacrifices of the continual burnt-offering represented atonement *provided*, whereas the individual sacrifices brought by the worshipers represented atonement *appropriated*.[14] For the continual burnt-offering, the so-called *tamidh*, was not primarily an expiatory sacrifice, rather, in common with all burnt-offerings, it was a sacrifice which typified the consecration of the worshiper to God. Thus this offering was better calculated to symbolize atonement *appropriated* than atonement *provided*. On the other hand, among the individual sacrifices brought by the worshipers in Old Testament times were the sin-offerings, aimed at providing expiation for sins whose effects terminated primarily on the individual himself, and the trespass-offerings which concerned sins whose effects terminated primarily on others. Since the basic idea behind both of these sacrifices was that of expiation and propitiation, these offerings certainly symbolized atonement *provided* much more vividly than atonement *appropriated*. So we see that the distinction Adventists make between these two types of offerings — a distinction which is basic to their doctrine

---

[12] C. F. Keil and F. Delitzsch, *Commentary on the Pentateuch*, trans. James Martin (Edinburgh: Clark, 1891), II, 395.

[13] *Ibid.*, p. 402. We could add that this communal sin-offering bore the same general relation to the individual offerings of the people that a congregational confession of sin on Sunday morning bears to the individual confessions of the members. Neither the ceremonies of the Day of Atonement nor the public confession of sin implies that the sins confessed individually were not previously forgiven and removed from God's record.

[14] *Questions on Doctrine*, p. 361.

of the investigative judgment — is also not in harmony with the facts.

(3) A third reason why the doctrine of the investigative judgment is to be rejected is that this doctrine *is based on a mistaken application of the Old Testament sacrificial system to Christ.* This, of course, naturally follows from the previous point. If Seventh-day Adventists misunderstand the Old Testament sacrificial system, it follows that they will also misapply that sacrificial system to the work of Christ. Let us now look at this matter in detail.

First, the Adventists mistakenly apply the Old Testament sacrificial system to Christ by insisting that Christ only forgave sins previous to 1844 but did not blot them out. It will be recalled that Crosier taught this in his *Day-Star* article (see above, p. 14), and that Seventh-day Adventists today still teach this (above, p. 41). This view ties in with their understanding of the meaning of the Old Testament sacrifices, as the following quotation will show:

> In the sanctuary in heaven, the record of sins is the only counterpart of the defilement of the earthly sanctuary. That the sins of men are recorded in heaven, we shall show in the next section. It is the expunging, or blotting out, of these sins from the heavenly records that fulfills the type set forth in the services on the Day of Atonement. In that way the sanctuary in heaven can be cleansed from all defilement.[15]

The thrust of these words is that, previous to 1844, the sins of penitent believers, though forgiven, were recorded in the heavenly sanctuary; it was not until after 1844 that the process of blotting out these sins was begun.

In refutation, we reply that the conception of sins being recorded in the sanctuary is one which has been shown to rest on a misunderstanding of the Old Testament sacrificial system. Further, the thought that Christ did not blot out sins previous to 1844 is without one shred of Scriptural support. On the contrary, David exclaims in Psalm 103:12, "As far as the east is from the west, so far hath he removed (*hirchiq,* Hiphil perfect of *rachaq,* indicating completed action) our transgressions from us."[16] In Isaiah 44:22 we read, "I have blotted out (*machithi,* perfect tense,

---

[15] *Questions on Doctrine,* p. 435.
[16] On p. 443 of *Questions on Doctrine* the authors admit that this figure is one used in Scripture to express the complete obliteration of sin.

indicating complete action), as a thick cloud, thy transgressions, and, as a cloud, thy sins. . . ." If in the Old Testament we are already told that God has blotted out the sins of His people, how can one say that Christ, the second Person of the Trinity, could not blot out sins in the New Testament era previous to 1844?

In fact, the entire distinction between the forgiveness of sins and the blotting out of sins — which is basic to Seventh-day Adventist theology — is foreign to the Scriptures. Does David suggest that there is any such distinction when he prays, in Psalm 51:1, "Have mercy upon me, O God, according to thy lovingkindness; According to the multitude of thy tender mercies blot out my transgressions"? In the New Testament the word commonly used for *forgive* is *aphieemi*. The root meaning of this word is to *let go* or to *send away*; hence it has acquired the additional meaning: to *cancel, remit,* or *pardon* sins.[17] Is there, now, any justification for the view that one's sin can be canceled without being blotted out? When Jesus, for example, said to the paralytic, "Son, be of good cheer; thy sins are forgiven" (Mt. 9:2), did He mean: your sins are now forgiven, but not yet blotted out; if you do not continue to live up to all my commandments, these sins may still be held against you? Why should the paralytic have been of good cheer, if this was the meaning of these words?

Seventh-day Adventists try to justify this distinction by appealing to the Parable of the Unmerciful Servant in Matthew 18:23-35. They contend that, since the king in the parable revoked his cancellation of the unmerciful servant's debt, God may also withdraw forgiveness once granted — hence the forgiveness of sins does not necessarily mean the blotting out of sins.[18] The flaw in this reasoning is that an earthly king cannot read hearts, whereas God can. The point of the parable is not that God may revoke forgiveness once bestowed, but that we must be ready to forgive others if we expect to be forgiven by God. Christ Himself expresses this point very clearly when He says, "For if ye forgive men their trespasses, your heavenly Father will also forgive you. But if ye forgive not men their trespasses, neither will your Father forgive your trespasses" (Mt. 6:14, 15). In other words, a man who does not forgive those who have sinned

---

[17] Arndt and Gingrich, *Greek-English Lexicon of the New Testament* (Chicago: University of Chicago Press, 1957), p. 125.
[18] *Questions on Doctrine,* pp. 439-40.

against him has *never really had his sins forgiven* by God, though he may think so.

We conclude that the Seventh-day Adventist distinction between the forgiveness of sin and the blotting out of sin is completely foreign to Scripture and robs the believer of all assurance of salvation.

Secondly, the idea that Christ has been engaged since 1844 in a work of investigative judgment in the heavenly sanctuary is completely without Biblical support. For, according to the Scriptures, the present work of Christ in heaven is a work of intercession, not a work of judging. Note, for example, how clearly this is taught in Hebrews 7:25, "Wherefore also he is able to save to the uttermost them that draw near unto God through him, seeing he ever liveth to make intercession for them." The basic meaning of the verb *entugchanoo,* which is here used, is to *plead for someone* or to *intercede for someone.*[19] The thought of judging, of examining records, of determining whether individuals are worthy of salvation or not, is completely foreign to this word. The same verb is used in Romans 8:34, "Who is he that condemneth? It is Christ Jesus that died, yea rather, that was raised from the dead, who is at the right hand of God, who also maketh intercession for us." In both passages, the verb *entugchanoo* is in the present tense, indicating that this intercession is a continuing activity. In Hebrews 7:25, in fact, the infinitive phrase *eis to entugchanein* shows that this intercession constitutes the very purpose for which Christ now lives! On what Scriptural ground, therefore, can Adventists say that Christ is now engaged in a work of judgment?[20]

It is, of course, true that there shall be a judgment of all men. But this judgment will occur after Christ has returned, not before. Note what our Lord Himself tells us, in Matthew 25:31-32, "But when the Son of man shall come in his glory, and all the angels with him, then shall he sit on the throne of his glory; and before him shall be gathered all the nations. . . ."

---

[19] Arndt and Gingrich, *op. cit.,* p. 269.
[20] Adventists grant that Christ is our Advocate and that He pleads the cases of His own people in the investigative judgment (*Questions on Doctrine,* pp. 441-42). Since, however, by their own definition, the work Christ is doing since 1844 is a work of *judgment,* we can only conclude that their theology evinces a serious confusion between Christ's work as Priest and Christ's work as Judge. How can He both plead the cases of His people and judge them at the same time?

Christ then goes on to describe the nature of this judgment and the standard whereby men shall be judged, ending his description with the familiar words, "And these shall go away into eternal punishment; but the righteous into eternal life" (v. 46). Here, indeed, we read about an "investigative judgment" — a judgment based on an investigation of the lives of those arraigned before the throne; but this judgment takes place after Christ has returned in glory. In II Thessalonians 1:7-9 we read: "And to you that are afflicted rest with us, at the revelation of the Lord Jesus from heaven with the angels of his power in flaming fire, rendering vengeance to them that know not God, and to them that obey not the gospel of our Lord Jesus: who shall suffer punishment, even eternal destruction from the face of the Lord. . . ." The work of Christ as judge is here pictured as occurring after His return from heaven. In Revelation 20:11-15 we also read about the judgment. It is described as being before the great white throne (v. 11), as involving all the dead (vv. 12 and 13) — this implies that the resurrection must have occurred before this time — and as being based on works (v. 12). At the end of this judgment, we are told, death and Hades are cast into the lake of fire (v. 14); from 21:4 we learn that the cessation of death shall be a mark of the final state. We also learn that those who are not found written in the book of life are cast into the lake of fire — this, too, is an event which points to the end of time. From every indication, therefore, we observe that the judgment here pictured is not one which is going on now, but one which will take place just before the final state is ushered in. From the other passages cited we conclude that this must be after Christ's return to earth.

What Scriptural warrant do Seventh-day Adventists have for teaching that there will be a judgment according to works before the return of Christ? The Scripture passages alluded to in parentheses at the end of Article 16 of the *Fundamental Beliefs* (an article dealing with the investigative judgment) do not give the slightest support for this doctrine. The first one, I Peter 4:17-18, "For the time is come for judgment to begin at the house of God," simply states, in harmony with the context, that Christians may often have to be chastised by God in this world in order that they may become more holy; it says nothing about any judgment in the heavenly sanctuary. The second passage, Daniel 7:9 and 10, pictures the Ancient of Days seated on a throne, and a judgment which involves the opening of books. This vision, however, which is to be understood in the light of the rest of the chapter, and particularly in the light of verses 13 and 14 (the giving of dominion and glory to the Son of Man), does not depict any investigative judgment in the heavenly sanctuary, but vividly symbolizes the overthrow of earthly empires and powers that are opposed to God and the establishment of Christ's everlasting reign. The third passage, Revelation 14:6-7, describes the message of the first angel: "Fear God, and give him glory; for the hour of his judgment is come." One needs a great deal of imagination to see in this verse a reference to an investigative judgment by Christ in the heavenly sanctuary! The last text mentioned is Luke 20:35, where Jesus is reported as saying, "But they that are accounted worthy to attain to that world, and the resurrection from the dead, neither marry, nor are given in marriage." Jesus is simply saying that those who will be privileged to enjoy the resurrection of believers will not marry; He gives not the slightest suggestion that their worthiness to attain this state will be determined by an investigative judgment in the heavenly sanctuary. Anyone who sees an investigative judgment taught in the verses just examined is seeing something in these passages which simply is not there!

(4) A fourth reason why the doctrine of the investigative judgment is to be rejected is *that it violates Scriptural teaching about the sovereignty of God.* It is clearly stated, in Article 16 of the *Fundamental Beliefs,* that "this investigative judgment determines who of the myriads sleeping in the dust of the earth are worthy of a part in the first resurrection, and who of its living multitudes are worthy of translation." This statement, however, stands in violent contradiction to what is said on page 420 of *Questions on Doctrine*: ". . . As Sovereign God, He . . . knows just who will accept and who will reject His 'great salvation.'" If this is so, why should God or Christ have to examine books of record to *determine* who may be raised in glory or translated into glory? Seventh-day Adventists cannot have their cake and eat it: either God does know who will accept His great salvation, and in that case the investigative judgment is unnecessary — or He must conduct an investigation to find out who is saved, and then He cannot be said to foreknow this!

Let us see what Mrs. White, the prophetess of Seventh-day Adventism, has to say about this matter:

> . . . There must be an examination of the books of record to determine who, through repentance of sin and faith in Christ, are entitled to the benefits of His atonement. The cleansing of the sanctuary therefore involves a work of investigation, — a work of judgment. This work must be performed prior to the coming of Christ to redeem His people; for when He comes, His reward is with Him to give to every man according to his works.[21]

This statement leaves us with a God who has to do homework before He can know who are entitled to the benefits of the atonement, and with a Christ who, like an earthly professor, must mark his examination papers before He knows what grade to give to each student! What resemblance is there between this God and this Christ on the one hand, and the God and Christ of the Scriptures on the other? We learn from Ephesians 1:4 that the destinies of the saved are not only foreknown by God but have been predetermined from eternity: "Even as he chose us in him [in Christ] before the foundation of the world." Crystal clear on this point is Romans 8:29-30: "For whom he foreknew, he also foreordained to be conformed to the image of his Son, that he might be the firstborn among many brethren; and whom he foreordained, them he also called; and whom he called, them he also justified; and whom he justified, them he also glorified." Why should God have to conduct an investigative judgment about those whom He has foreordained from eternity to be justified and glorified?

What about Christ? The Bible tells us that Christ knows His sheep, and has given them eternal life, so that no one can snatch them out of His hand (Jn. 10:27-28); that He prayed not for the world but for those whom the Father had given Him (John 17:9); that it is the will of Him that sent Christ that of all that which the Father had given Him He should lose nothing, but should raise it up at the last day (Jn. 6:39). Does this Christ, now, have to conduct an investigation to determine which of the inhabitants of the earth shall be raised in glory?

Adventists try to get around this difficulty by saying:

[21] *The Great Controversy,* p. 422.

> Were God alone concerned, there would be no need of an investigation of the life records of men in this judgment [the investigative judgment], for as our eternal Sovereign God, He is omniscient. . . . But that the inhabitants of the whole universe, the good and evil angels, and all who have ever lived on this earth might understand His love and His justice, the life history of every individual who has ever lived on the earth has been recorded, and in the judgment [the investigative judgment] these records will be disclosed.[22]

But here is confusion worse confounded! In the first place, the above statement is not consistent with the assertion previously quoted, that the purpose of the investigative judgment is to *determine* who are worthy of resurrection to glory and translation. Further, what is said above makes sense if we think of the final judgment, which is public, in which the reasons for the final destinies of men will be made known to all. But it makes no sense when applied to the investigative judgment, which is not public, and which is therefore not witnessed by men!

(5) A fifth reason why the doctrine of the investigative judgment is to be rejected is that *it jeopardizes the Biblical teaching that we are saved by grace alone.* We have already touched upon this point (see above, pp. 49-52). Let us look at this matter a bit more closely. Mrs. White describes those who "pass" in the investigative judgment as follows:

> All who have truly repented of sin, and by faith claimed the blood of Christ as their atoning sacrifice, have had pardon entered against their names in the books of heaven; as they have become partakers of the righteousness of Christ, and their characters are found to be in harmony with the law of God, their sins will be blotted out, and they themselves will be accounted worthy of eternal life.[23]

The stipulation that the characters of these individuals must be found to be in harmony with the law of God before their sins can be blotted out suggests that they must have attained a certain legal righteousness of their own before they will receive full salvation.

In a chapter in which he discusses the investigative judgment, William Henry Branson says:

---

[22] *Questions on Doctrine*, pp. 420-21.
[23] *The Great Controversy*, p. 483, quoted in *Questions on Doctrine*, p. 443.

A Christian who through faith in Jesus Christ has faithfully kept the law's requirements will be acquitted [in the investigative judgment]; there is no condemnation, for the law finds no fault in him. If, on the other hand, it is found that one has broken even a single precept, and this transgression is unconfessed, he will be dealt with just as if he had broken all ten.[24]

In this astounding statement a prominent Seventh-day Adventist writer tells us that the basis for acquittal in the investigative judgment is the perfect keeping of the law's requirements! This is surely a far cry from the Apostle Paul's assertion, "We reckon therefore that a man is justified by faith apart from the works of the law" (Rom. 3:28). To the Galatians, who were being tempted to base their hope for salvation in part on works which they did themselves, came Paul's stern warning: "Ye are severed from Christ, ye who would be justified by the law; ye are fallen away from grace" (Gal. 5:4). If the determining factor in being accepted in the investigative judgment is the faithfulness with which one has kept the law's requirements, then certainly salvation is no longer by grace alone. And if the failure to confess even a single transgression of the law will result in damnation, one wonders what will happen to the Psalmist who exclaimed, "Who can discern his errors?" (Ps. 19:12). We conclude that the Seventh-day Adventist doctrine of the investigative judgment does not permit Adventists to continue to claim that they teach salvation by grace alone.

## THE SCAPEGOAT DOCTRINE

The other aspect of Seventh-day Adventist teaching in relation to the investigative judgment that remains to be evaluated is the view that the sins of mankind will be laid on Satan just before Christ's return to earth. It is my conviction that this doctrine, too, is completely without Scriptural support. For this judgment I advance the following four reasons:

(1) It is not at all certain that the word *Azazel* in Leviticus 16:8, and following verses, means Satan. Seventh-day Adventists insist that this is what the word means, citing a number of authorities to support their claim.[25] The plain fact of the matter, however, is that no one knows exactly what this strange word means. The early tradition rendered the word *la'aza'zeel* as fol-

---

[24] *Drama of the Ages*, p. 351.
[25] *Questions on Doctrine*, pp. 391-95.

lows: "for removal." The Septuagint translation of this expression was *too apopompaioo*: for the one to be sent away. From this was derived the Vulgate translation, *capro emissario*: for the goat to be sent forth. It is from this tradition that the King James rendering originated: "scapegoat" (literally, "escape-goat"). This ancient tradition still has many supporters. The Brown-Driver-Briggs Hebrew lexicon suggests that the word Azazel means "entire removal." The article on Azazel found in the *International Standard Bible Encyclopedia* suggests the same interpretation.[26] Others, however, argue from the juxtaposition of Azazel with Jahwe that the former must be a proper name. Following this interpretation, some hold that it must refer to Satan, and others suggest that it designates a wilderness demon. One must simply confess that, until further light is given, no one can be dogmatic as to the meaning of this word. It may mean Satan, but it may also mean something else.

(2) Even if it be granted, for the sake of argument, that Azazel does mean Satan, it does not at all follow that the second goat in the ceremonies of the Day of Atonement stood for Satan. For it is specifically stated in Leviticus 16:10 that the second goat was to be sent into the wilderness *la'aza'zeel*: *to* or *for* Azazel. If Azazel means Satan, the second goat was sent *to* or *for* Satan; to say that the second goat *stood for Satan* is to make an unwarranted leap from the entity to whom or for whom the goat was sent to the goat himself.

(3) It is, further, impossible to regard the second goat as standing for Satan since, according to Leviticus 16:5, the two goats represented one sin-offering. In the last-named verse we read, "And he [the high priest] shall take of the congregation of the children of Israel two he-goats for a sin-offering (*lechatta'th*)." It is not just the slain goat, in other words, that constitutes the sin-offering; it is the two goats together. This means that both goats pictured the propitiation that was to be offered by Christ. The slain goat pictured the fact that Christ was to shed His blood to redeem us from sin, whereas the goat sent into the wilderness pictured the fact that by His atoning work Christ was to remove our sins from us. To suggest, as Seventh-day Adventists do, that the second goat stood for Satan is to transfer a work of Christ to the Prince of Darkness!

[26] Ed. James Orr (rev. ed., Grand Rapids: Eerdmans, 1939), I, 342-44.

Note what Fairbairn has to say about this second goat:

> What took place with the live goat was merely intended to unfold, and render palpably evident to the bodily eye, the effect of the great work of atonement. The atonement itself was made in secret, while the high priest alone was in the sanctuary; and yet . . . it was of the utmost importance that there should be a visible transaction, like that of the dismissal of the scape-goat, embodying in a sensible form the results of the service. Nor is it of any moment what became of the goat after being conducted into the wilderness. It was enough that he was led into the region of drought and desolation, where . . . he should never more be seen or heard of. With such a destination, he was obviously as much a doomed victim as the one whose life-blood had already been shed and brought within the veil; he . . . exhibited a most striking image of the everlasting oblivion into which the sins of God's people are thrown, when once they are covered with the blood of an acceptable atonement.[27]

(4) That Satan will be punished for his sins is certainly taught in Scripture, but that our sins or the sins of all men will be placed on Satan is nowhere taught in Scripture. This idea rests, as we have just seen, on a misunderstanding of the role of the second goat in the ceremonies of the Day of Atonement. Further, this conception is in direct conflict with I Peter 2:24, where we read the following concerning Christ: "Who his own self bare our sins in his body upon the tree. . . ." It was therefore Christ who bore our sins and thus removed them; not Satan. To suggest that Christ still has to take our sins from the heavenly sanctuary at the end of time in order to lay them on Satan implies that He has not previously borne them away, and that His atoning work was therefore inadequate for the complete removal of sin. More-over, if Christ lays the sins of unbelievers on Satan as well, why must they still suffer for them? If, on the other hand, they do suffer for them, why must *their sins* still be laid on Satan? Finally, if it is necessary for these sins to be laid on Satan before they can be obliterated from the universe, Satan plays an indispensable part in the blotting out of sin. Though Seventh-day Adventists deny that Satan makes atonement for our sins in any way, they

---

[27] *Typology of Scripture,* II, 340-41. Cf. also W. Moeller in the *I. S. B. E.* article referred to above: "Both goats . . . represent two sides of the same thing. The second is necessary to make clear what the first one, which has been slain, can no longer represent, namely, the removal of the sin. . ." (I, 343).

are nevertheless guilty of ascribing something to Satan which should only be ascribed to Christ: the obliteration of our sins.

We conclude that the doctrines of the investigative judgment and of the laying of sins on Satan are false teachings. Not only do they lack all Scriptural support; they actually go contrary to Scripture at various points, as has been shown. If Seventh-day Adventists honestly wish to be true to Scripture alone in their teachings, they should repudiate both of these doctrines.[28]

[28] The reader is further referred to Herbert Bird's *Theology of Seventh-day Adventism,* pp. 72-92, and to Norman F. Douty's *Another Look at Seventh-day Adventism,* pp. 118-29, for competent evaluations of both the investigative judgment doctrine and the scapegoat teaching.

# V. Appendix B: Seventh-day Adventist Teaching on the Sabbath

In Chapter 3 we discussed the teaching of Seventh-day Adventists on the Sabbath insofar as it is inconsistent with their claim that they believe in salvation by grace alone (above, pp. 51-52). In this appendix we shall examine and evaluate their teaching on the question of the proper day to be observed by Christians. Are Seventh-day Adventists right in insisting that the seventh day of the week is the only proper Lord's day for us to observe, in obedience to the Fourth Commandment?

Here again we must first of all recall how their doctrine of the Sabbath originated. A retired sea captain (Joseph Bates) became convinced through reading an article in a periodical that the seventh day was the proper Sabbath to be kept. After having arrived at this conclusion, he came into contact with a group of Adventists in New Hampshire who had been influenced by a lay woman (Mrs. Rachel Oakes) to keep the seventh-day Sabbath. Having thus been confirmed in his convictions, Bates wrote two tracts about the Sabbath, in which the position still held by Seventh-day Adventists today was set forth (see above, pp. 15-16). In 1847, beween the publication of Bates's first and second tracts, Mrs. White had a vision in which she was taken into the holy of holies of the heavenly sanctuary, and saw the Ten Commandments with a halo of glory around the Sabbath Commandment (above, p. 18). We see, therefore, that the denomination arrived at its view about the Sabbath not through thorough, basic Bible study on the part of well-trained Biblical

89

scholars, but through the influence of non-theologically trained lay members and through a confirmatory vision from Mrs. White. It is on the basis of this type of "guidance" that Seventh-day Adventists overthrow the first-day Sunday, which has been observed by all the churches of Christendom since the beginning of the Christian era.

Let us look at some of the arguments Adventists advance for their position.

(1) *They maintain that the Sabbath is a memorial of creation,* that it had no ceremonial significance by foreshadowing something yet to come, but that it had only commemorative significance, pointing back to the creation of the world.[1] Since God created the world in six days and rested on the seventh day, the seventh-day-ness of the Sabbath was not a temporary feature of the day which was later to be changed, but always remained part of the Sabbath commandment.[2]

In answer to this argument, it should be observed that the Bible itself indicates that the Sabbath points forward as well as backward. In the fourth chapter of Hebrews a comparison is made between the rest of the Sabbath Day and the rest of heavenly glory. The inspired author is referring to future heavenly blessedness when he says, in verse 9, "There remaineth therefore a sabbath rest (*sabbatismos*) for the people of God." Obviously, therefore, the Sabbath is a type of heavenly rest, and does not have *merely* commemorative significance.

As far as the seventh-day-ness of the Sabbath is concerned, the very fact that the day was changed in New Testament times to the first day indicates that the seventh-day-ness was not an irrevocable aspect of the Sabbath commandment.[3]   Geerhardus Vos, while agreeing with the Adventists that the Sabbath has its roots in creation rather than in the Mosaic ordinance, and is therefore binding upon all mankind,[4] adds that the coming of Christ has brought about a change in the order in which the day of rest is observed:

> The universal Sabbath law received a modified significance under the Covenant of Grace.  The work which issues into the rest can no longer be man's own work.  It becomes the work

---

[1] *Questions on Doctrine,* p. 158.
[2] *Ibid.,* pp. 161-65.
[3] The evidence supporting this statement will be given later in this appendix.
[4] *Biblical Theology* (Grand Rapids, Eerdmans, 1954), p. 155.

of Christ. This the Old Testament and the New Testament have in common. But they differ as to the perspective in which they each see the emergence of work and rest. Inasmuch as the Old Covenant was still looking forward to the performance of the Messianic work, naturally the days of labor to it come first, the day of rest falls at the end of the week. We, under the New Covenant, look back upon the accomplished work of Christ. We, therefore, first celebrate the rest in principle procured by Christ, although the Sabbath also still remains a sign looking forward to the final eschatological rest.[5]

The position of the historic Christian church on this matter is well set forth in the Westminster Confession of Faith:

> As it is of the law of nature, that, in general, a due proportion of time be set apart for the worship of God; so, in his Word, by a positive, moral, and perpetual commandment, binding all men in all ages, he hath particularly appointed one day in seven for a Sabbath, to be kept holy unto him (Ex. 20:8, 10, 11; Isa. 56:2, 4, 6, 7): which, from the beginning of the world to the resurrection of Christ, was the last day of the week; and, from the resurrection of Christ, was changed into the first day of the week (Gen. 2:2, 3; I Cor. 16:1, 2; Acts 20:7), which in Scripture is called the Lord's day (Rev. 1:10), and is to be continued to the end of the world, as the Christian Sabbath (Ex. 20:8, 10, with Mt. 5:17, 18).[6]

(2) Seventh-day Adventists *cite Revelation 14 to buttress their position on the Sabbath*: "We believe that the restoration of the Sabbath is indicated in the Bible prophecy of Revelation 14:9-12."[7] On another page the authors of *Questions on Doctrine* affirm that they understand the prophecies of Daniel 7 and Revelation 13 relating to the beast to have reference particularly to the Papacy, adding,

> Thus it was that the Adventist heralds of Sabbath reform came to make a further logical application of the mark of the

---

5 *Ibid.,* pp. 157-158.

6 Chap. 21, Section 7, as found in Schaff's *Creeds of Christendom,* 4th ed. (New York: Harper, 1919), III, 648-49. The *Post Acta* of the Synod of Dort of 1618-19 contain a statement about Sabbath observance which distinguishes between a ceremonial element and a moral element in the Fourth Commandment. The ceremonial element, which has been abolished for New Testament Christians, is the observance of the seventh day. The moral element, which is still binding, is the observance of a definite day for rest and worship. This statement, which has been adopted by the Christian Reformed Church, may be found in J. L. Schaver's *Polity of the Churches* (Chicago: Church Polity Press, 1947), II, 33.

7 *Questions on Doctrine,* p. 153.

beast — holding it to be, in essence, the attempted change of the Sabbath of the fourth commandment of the Decalogue by the Papacy, its endeavor to impose this change on Christendom, and the acceptance of the Papacy's substitute by individuals.[8]

The reader's attention is now called to the text of Revelation 14:9-12:

> And another angel, a third, followed them, saying with a great voice, If any man worshippeth the beast and his image, and receiveth a mark on his forehead, or upon his hand, he also shall drink of the wine of the wrath of God, which is prepared unmixed in the cup of his anger; and he shall be tormented with fire and brimstone in the presence of the holy angels, and in the presence of the Lamb: and the smoke of their torment goeth up for ever and ever; and they have no rest day and night, they that worship the beast and his image, and whoso receiveth the mark of his name. Here is the patience of the saints, they that keep the commandments of God, and the faith of Jesus.

Where, now, does one see any reference to the Sabbath in this entire passage? One can perhaps excuse a retired sea captain for imagining that he could see a denunciation of the first-day Sabbath in this passage, but for an entire denomination to adopt this interpretation is a far more serious matter. By this type of irresponsible exegesis one can prove anything from the Bible which he wishes to.

(3) Seventh-day Adventists assert that *the New Testament emphasizes the observance of the seventh day as the Sabbath.* For proof they point to the fact that both Jesus[9] and Paul[10] observed the seventh day rather than the first. This argument, however, is not difficult to meet. Our Lord observed the seventh day before His resurrection because He was at that time bound to the Old Testament regulation. It is significant to note, however, that *after* His resurrection He appeared to the apostles on two successive first days of the week. As far as the Apostle Paul is concerned, he went to Jewish synagogues on the seventh-day Sabbath because he wished to witness to Jews, whom he could find there on that

---

8 *Ibid.*, p. 181.
9 *Ibid.*, p. 151, 161.
10 Arthur E. Lickey, *God Speaks to Modern Man* (Review and Herald, 1952), pp. 424, 430. On the latter page Lickey makes the point that Luke, in the book of Acts, recorded eighty-four Sabbath services and only one first-day meeting for worship.

day. Does the fact that Seventh-day Adventists sometimes attend Sunday church services in order to win converts to their faith imply that they believe the first day of the week to be the Sabbath? Further, it is to be remembered that Paul did address a gathering of Christians at Troas on the first day of the week — to this point we shall come back in a moment.

What proof is there now from the New Testament itself that the observance of the Sabbath was changed from the seventh to the first day of the week? Let us note the following Biblical facts:

(i) Jesus arose from the dead on the first day of the week (John 20:1), thus designating the first day as the one now to be observed.[11]

(ii) Jesus appeared to ten of His disciples on the evening of that first day of the week (John 20:19ff.).

(iii) On the following first day of the week, Jesus appeared to the eleven disciples (John 20:26ff.).

(iv) The promised coming of the Holy Spirit was fulfilled on the first day of the week (Acts 2:1ff.). Since this was an event of as great importance as the incarnation of Christ, it is highly significant that this outpouring occurred on a Sunday.[12]

(v) On that same first day of the week the first gospel sermon was preached by Peter (Acts 2:14ff.), and 3,000 converts were received into the church (Acts 2:41).

(vi) At Troas the Christians of that city assembled for worship on the first day of the week and Paul preached to them (Acts 20:

---

[11] Even Seventh-day Adventists admit that Christ arose on the first day (*Questions on Doctrine*, p. 151). Vos, quoting Delitzsch, makes the comment that, since Christ lay in the grave on the seventh day, the Jewish Sabbath was, as it were, buried in His grave (*op. cit.*, p. 158).

[12] The question might be asked, How do we know that the day of Pentecost mentioned in Acts 2 fell on a Sunday? The word *Penteekostee* which is here used means "fiftieth." It designated the Jewish Feast of Weeks, at which two wave-loaves of leavened bread were offered to the Lord. Lev. 23:15-16 specified that this feast was to be observed on the morrow after the seventh Sabbath after the Feast of the Passover. The Sadducean party in the first century A.D. interpreted "the morrow after the Sabbath" as being a first day of the week; on this interpretation Pentecost would always fall on a Sunday. The Pharisees of that day, however, interpreted the Leviticus passage in such a way that Pentecost fell on various days of the week. F. F. Bruce points out that, though the Pharisaic interpretation became normative for Judaism after A.D. 70, "While the temple stood, their [the Sadducees'] interpretation would be normative for the public celebration of the festival [Pentecost]; Christian tradition is therefore right in fixing the anniversary of the descent of the Spirit on a Sunday" (*Commentary on the Book of the Acts* [Grand Rapids: Eerdmans, 1955], p. 53, n. 3).

6-7). With respect to this passage a leading Seventh-day Adventist writer says,

> The first day of the week (Bible time) begins Saturday night at sundown and ends Sunday night at sundown. Inasmuch as this meeting was held on the first day of the week and at night, it must therefore have been on what we call Saturday night, the first day having begun at sundown.[13]

Lickey's reasoning assumes that Luke was following the Jewish system of reckoning, which began a day at sundown. F. F. Bruce, however, contends that Luke was not using the Jewish mode of reckoning, but the Roman reckoning from midnight to midnight;[14] on this basis Luke was designating, not Saturday evening, but Sunday evening. Lickey further contends that this meeting was not a regular service but simply a farewell meeting for Paul, and that it therefore tells us nothing about the day on which Christians ordinarily met for worship.[15] To this it may be replied that Luke's statement, "we being gathered together to break bread" strongly suggests (though it does not finally prove) the thought that this was a regular meeting at which they ate together and celebrated the Lord's Supper.[16] If there was no special significance in the day on which the Christians met, why should Luke take the trouble to say, as he does, "on the first day of the week"? This item of information could well have been omitted if it conveyed a fact of no importance. That Luke mentions it shows that already at this time Christians were gathering for worship on the first day of the week.

(vii) Paul instructed the Christians at Corinth to make contributions for the poor in Jerusalem on the first day of the week: "Upon the first day of the week let each one of you lay by him in store, as he may prosper, that no collections be made when I come" (I Cor. 16:2). As can be imagined, Adventists find in this passage no proof for the observance of the first day as a day of worship. M. L. Andreasen, for example, contends that this passage does not refer to a collection taken in church, but that it

---

13 Lickey, *op. cit.*, p. 430.
14 *Op. cit.*, p. 408, n. 25. Cf. O. Cullmann, *Early Christian Worship* (London, 1953), pp. 10ff., 88ff. In either case, however, the meeting was held on the first day of the week.
15 *Op. cit.*, p. 431. Cf. M. L. Andreasen, *The Sabbath, Which Day and Why?* (Washington: Review and Herald, 1942), pp. 167-70.
16 Bruce, *op. cit.*, p. 408. Cf. R. C. H. Lenski, *Acts of the Apostles* (Columbus: Wartburg Press, 1944), p. 826; also F. W. Grosheide, *Handelingen*, in *Korte Verklaring* (Kampen: Kok, 1950), p. 107.

instructs the Corinthian Christians to lay aside money at home, as they had been prospered; this would involve some bookkeeping, which would be inappropriate on the Sabbath — hence Paul instructs them to do this on Sunday.[17] Lickey advances a similar interpretation, saying, among other things,

> A church member runs a small shop all week, let us say. Friday afternoon he closes early enough to prepare for the Sabbath. There is no time to figure accounts. But when the Sabbath is past, and the first day of the week comes, he is to check his net earnings and lay aside a proper sum, not at church, but at home.[18]

We shall have to agree that Paul is here probably not speaking of an offering which is to be taken at a church service. The expression *par' heautoo tithetoo* is in all likelihood to be understood as meaning: let him lay aside by himself — that is, at home.[19] Again, however, it is important to note that the first day of the week is specifically designated for this laying aside. Why should Paul say this if the Corinthians regularly gathered for worship on Saturday? Christian giving is part of our worship; it is to be expected that we engage in this form of worship on the day on which we gather for public prayers. Surely not every member of the Corinthian church was a shopkeeper who needed to do some figuring before he could determine how much he should give; surely, also, even the shopkeepers could do their figuring on the evening before the day of worship as well as on the day after. The only plausible reason for mentioning the first day in this passage is that this was the customary day on which Christians were meeting for worship.[20]

(viii) The Apostle John wrote, in Revelation 1:10, "I was in the Spirit on the Lord's day (*en tee kuriakee heemera*). The Greek word *kuriakee* is an adjective meaning "belonging to the

17 *The Sabbath*, pp. 172-74.
18 *Op. cit.*, pp. 433-34.
19 It is so understood by Grosheide, in his *Commentary on First Corinthians* (Eerdmans, 1955), p. 398; by Lenski in his *First Corinthians* (Columbus: Wartburg Press, 1946), p. 759; and by Arndt and Gingrich in their *Greek-English Lexicon*, p. 615 (though qualified by a *probably*). Charles Hodge, however, is of the opinion that Paul is referring to an offering brought to church and collected there (*First Corinthians* [Eerdmans. reprinted 1956], pp. 363-64).
20 So also Grosheide, Lenski, and Hodge, in the works mentioned above.

Lord"; literally, therefore, the expression means: *on the day belonging to the Lord.* Seventh-day Adventists contend that the
expression *the Lord's day,* as here used, refers to Saturday.[21] In
taking this position, however, they stand completely alone. These
words have been understood universally as referring to Sunday,
the first day of the week. They are so understood by the standard
commentators, and by the standard lexicons.[22] If we add to this
the fact that the expression is used to stand for Sunday in such
early Christian writings as the *Didachee* and Ignatius's *Letter to the
Magnesians,* we see on what flimsy grounds Adventists stand when
they try to interpret these words as meaning Saturday. John's
statement that he was in the Spirit on the Lord's Day further con-
firms the fact that the first day of the week was now the one commonly used for worship.[23]

(4) Seventh-day Adventists contend that "*the earliest authentic
instance, in early church writings, of the first day of the week
being called 'Lord's Day' was by Clement of Alexandria, near the
close of the second century.*"[24] That this statement is quite contrary to fact will be evident from the following quotations:

(i) Revelation 1:10, "I was in the Spirit on the Lord's Day."[25]

(ii) From the Epistle of Ignatius *To the Magnesians,* Section 9:
"If then those who had walked in ancient practices attained unto
newness of hope, no longer observing sabbaths, but fashioning

21 Lickey, *op. cit.,* p. 415; and Andreasen, *The Sabbath,* p. 186.

22 Under the latter the following may be mentioned: Moulton and
Milligan, *Vocabulary of the Greek Testament* (Eerdmans, 1957), p.
364; Werner Foerster, in Kittel's *Theologisches Woerterbuch zum Neuen
Testament* (Stuttgart: Kohlhammer, 1938), III, 1096; and Arndt and
Gingrich's *Greek-English Lexicon,* p. 459. The last-named authors say,
under Lord's day: "Certainly Sunday (so in Modern Greek)."

23 The book of Revelation was probably written during the last decade
of the first century. Thus we have seen evidence that the first day
of the week was being used as the day of worship by Christians as
early as the first century. If, now, this was contrary to the will of God,
the Apostles should have opposed its use and warned Christians against
it. We find no such opposition, however; on the contrary, we find Paul
supporting the first day by urging Christians to lay aside their gifts on
that day.

24 *Questions on Doctrine,* p. 166. The reference given in Clement
is *Miscellanies,* V, 14.

25 Written about A.D. 95. See above discussion.

their lives after the Lord's day, on which our life also arose through him. . . ."[26]

(iii) From the *Didachee*, or *Teaching of the Twelve Apostles,* Section 14: "And on the Lord's Day gather yourselves together and break bread and give thanks. . . ."[27]

(Though the following two quotations do not use the expression, "the Lord's Day," they do give further evidence for the early observance of the first day of the week as the day of worship.)

(iv) From the *Epistle of Barnabas,* Section 15: "Wherefore also we keep the eighth day for rejoicing, in the which also Jesus rose from the dead, and having been manifested ascended into the heavens."[28]

(v) From Justin Martyr's *First Apology,* Chapter 67: "But Sunday is the day on which we all hold our common assembly, because it is the first day on which God, having wrought a change in the darkness and matter, made the world; and Jesus Christ our Saviour on the same day rose from the dead."[29]

The statements quoted above, plus the New Testament evidence previously given, make it quite evident that the change from the

[26] Written about A.D. 107. Text from J. B. Lightfoot's *The Apostolic Fathers* (Grand Rapids: Baker, 1956), p. 71.
[27] Written during the last part of the first century or the beginning of the second. Text from Lightfoot, *op. cit.,* p. 128.
[28] Written some time between 70 and 130 A.D. Text from Lightfoot, *op. cit.,* p. 152.
[29] Written about 155 A.D. Text from *The Ante-Nicene Fathers* (Eerdmans, reprinted 1956), I, 186. Seventh-day Adventists contend that what Justin speaks of here was a "festival of the resurrection" which began to be observed alongside of the seventh-day Sabbath from the middle of the second century (*Questions on Doctrine,* p. 152). This, however, seems very unlikely. The service held on this day, as described in the earlier part of the chapter, includes Scripture reading, a brief homily, prayer, thanksgiving, the celebration of the Lord's Supper, and an offering for the needy. This certainly appears to be a description of a regular Sunday worship service. If this were a festival service held alongside of Sabbath worship, one would expect some reference to this fact in the chapter. No such reference is found, however; instead, Justin says: "Sunday is the day on which we all hold *our common assembly. . . .*" Further, in the *Dialogue with Trypho,* written some time after the *First Apology,* Justin clearly affirms that the Gentile Christians of his day did not observe the Sabbath: "But the Gentiles, who have believed on Him [Christ] . . . they shall receive the inheritance . . . even although they neither keep the Sabbath, nor are circumcised, nor observe the feasts" (Chap. 26; text from *The Ante-Nicene Fathers,* I, 207).

seventh day to the first day was not brought about by "the Papacy," as Seventh-day Adventism contends,[30] but came about long before the Papacy arose as a strong ecclesiastical institution. We conclude that the Adventist position on the Sabbath is not only historically unwarranted, but is also without Scriptural support.[31]

[30] *Questions on Doctrine*, p. 181. We are never told, however, exactly which Pope it was who changed the day.

[31] For further treatment and elaboration of the subject discussed in this appendix, the reader is referred to Bird's *Theology of Seventh-Day Adventism*, pp. 93-118; Douty's *Another Look at Seventh-day Adventism*, pp. 80-91; and Martin's *The Truth About Seventh-day Adventism*, pp. 140-73. Older but very thorough is D. M. Canright's *The Lord's Day from Neither Catholics Nor Pagans*, subtitled "An Answer to Seventh-day Adventists on this Subject" (New York: Revell, 1915). Valuable material may also be found in J. K. Van Baalen's *Chaos of Cults*, 4th ed. (Eerdmans, 1962), pp. 240-47, 249-53.

# Bibliography

PRIMARY SOURCES:

White, Ellen Gould. *Patriarchs and Prophets.* Mountain View, Calif.: Pacific Press Pub. Association, 1913 (first pub. in 1890). (Vol. I of the Conflict of the Ages Series).

————. *Prophets and Kings.* Mountain View: Pacific Press, 1917. (Vol. II of the Conflict of the Ages Series).

————. *The Desire of Ages.* Mountain View: Pacific Press, 1940 (first pub. in 1898). (Vol. III of the Conflict of the Ages Series).

————. *The Acts of the Apostles in the Proclamation of the Gospel of Jesus Christ.* Mountain View: Pacific Press, 1947 (first pub. in 1911). (Vol. IV of the Conflict of the Ages Series).

————. *The Great Controversy Between Christ and Satan.* Mountain View: Pacific Press, 1911 (first pub. in 1888). (Vol. V of the Conflict of the Ages Series).

————. *Christ's Object Lessons.* Washington, D.C.: Review and Herald Pub. Association, 1941. A discussion of the parables of Jesus.

————. *Counsels on Stewardship.* Washington, D.C.: Review and Herald, 1940.

————. *Education.* Mountain View: Pacific Press, 1942 (first pub. in 1903).

————. *Gospel Workers.* Washington, D.C.: Review and Herald, 1915.

————. *The Ministry of Healing.* Mountain View: Pacific Press, 1942 (first pub. in 1905).

————. *The Sanctified Life.* Washington, D.C.: Review and Herald, 1937.

————. *Steps to Christ.* Washington, D.C.: Review and Herald, 1921 (first pub. in 1892).

————. *Testimonies for the Church.* Vols. I-IX (1855-1909).

————. *Thoughts from the Mount of Blessing.* Mountain View: Pacific Press, 1928 (first pub. in 1896).

HISTORIES OF SEVENTH-DAY ADVENTISM:

Department of Education, General Conference of Seventh-day Adventists. *The Story of Our Church.* Mountain View: Pacific Press, 1960 (copyrighted in 1956). An official, though popularized, history.

Froom, Leroy Edwin. *The Prophetic Faith of Our Fathers.* The Historical Development of Prophetic Interpretation. 4 vols. Washington, D.C.: Review and Herald, 1946-54. A voluminous study of the history of the interpretation of prophecy. Vol. IV contains the history of the beginnings of the Seventh-day Adventist denomination.

Loughborough, John N. *Rise and Progress of the Seventh-day Adventists.* Battle Creek: General Conference Association of Seventhday Adventists, 1892.

————. *The Great Second Advent Movement.* Washington, D.C.: Review and Herald, 1909.

Nichol, Francis D. *The Midnight Cry.* Washington, D. C.: Review and Herald, 1945. A defense of the character and conduct of Wm. Miller and the Millerites.

Olsen, Mahlon E. *A History of the Origin and Progress of Seventhday Adventists.* 2nd ed. Washington, D. C.: Review and Herald, 1926.

Spalding, Arthur W. *Captains of the Host.* Washington, D.C.: Review and Herald, 1949. A history of Seventh-day Adventism up to 1900.

————. *Christ's Last Legion.* Washington, D.C.: Review and Herald, 1949. The history of Seventh-day Adventism since 1900.


SEVENTH-DAY ADVENTIST PUBLICATIONS:

Andreasen, M. L. *God's Holy Day.* Washington, D. C.: Review and Herald, 1949.

————. *The Sabbath, Which Day and Why?* Washington, D. C.: Review and Herald, 1942.

————. *The Sanctuary Service.* 2nd ed., rev. Washington, D. C.: Review and Herald, 1947.

*Bible Readings for the Home.* Rev. ed. Washington, D. C.: Review and Herald, 1949.

Branson, Wm. H. *In Defense of the Faith.* Washington, D. C.: Review and Herald, 1933. A reply to Canright's book, *Seventhday Adventism Renounced.*

————. *The Drama of the Ages.* Nashville: Southern Pub. Association, 1950. God's plan for saving man from sin.

Department of Education, General Conference of Seventh-day Adventists. *Principles of Life from the Word of God.* A Systematic Study of the Major Doctrines of the Bible. Mountain View:

Pacific Press, 1952 (4th printing, 1960). Intended for classroom use.

Graybill, Ronald D. *E. G. White and Church Race Relations.* Washington, D.C.: Review and Herald, 1970. Presents evidence from Mrs. White's writings that she believed in the equality of the races.

————. *Mission to Black America.* Mountain View: Pacific Press, 1971. A history of work among southern Negroes by James Edson White, son of Ellen G. White.

Haynes, Carlyle B. *The Christian Sabbath.* Nashville: Southern Pub. Assn., 1949.

————. *Life, Death, and Immortality.* Nashville: Southern Pub. Assn., 1952.

————. *Our Lord's Return.* Nashville: Southern Pub. Assn., 1948.

————. *Seventh-day Adventists, their Work and Teachings.* Washington, D. ·C.: Review and Herald, 1940. Discusses major doctrines, activities, finances, institutions, leadership, customs.

Lickey, Arthur E. *Fundamentals of the Everlasting Gospel.* Washington, D. C.: Review and Herald, 1947. Brief statement of fundamental beliefs, suitable for the instruction of converts.

————. *God Speaks to Modern Man.* Washington, D. C.: Review and Herald, 1952. A rather thorough discussion of Adventist teachings.

Nichol, Francis D. *Answers to Objections.* Washington, D. C.: Review and Herald, 1952. Contains some of the material found in *Reasons for our Faith,* but has much additional material. An extensive work.

————. *Ellen G. White and her Critics.* Washington, D. C.: Review and Herald, 1951. An attempt to answer various criticisms of Mrs. White.

————. *Questions People Have Asked Me.* Washington, D. C.: Review and Herald, 1959. The questions concern ethical, practical, and doctrinal problems.

————. *Reasons for our Faith.* Washington, D. C.: Review and Herald, 1947. Discusses questions vital to the proper understanding and effective presentation of certain Adventist teachings.

*Seventh-day Adventist Bible Dictionary.* Don F. Neufeld, ed. Authors: Siegfried H. Horn, et. al. Washington, D. C.: Review and Herald, 1960.

*Seventh-day Adventist Bible Commentary.* Francis D. Nichol, ed. 7 vols. Washington, D. C.: Review and Herald, 1953-57. Contains general articles on doctrinal and Biblical topics, as well as a verse-by-verse commentary.

*Seventh-day Adventist Church Manual.* General Conference of Seventh-day Adventists, 1959. Beliefs, church government, membership, duties of officers, services and meetings, auxiliary organizations, finances, standards of Christian living, church discipline.

*Seventh-day Adventists Answer Questions on Doctrine.* An Explanation of Certain Major Aspects of Seventh-day Adventist Belief. Prepared by a Representative Group of Seventh-day Adventist Leaders, Bible Teachers, and Editors. Washington, D. C.: Review and Herald, 1957. Contains answers to questions submitted to the denomination by Walter R. Martin. It may be considered the most recent official statement of Seventh-day Adventist doctrine.

Smith, Uriah. *The Prophecies of Daniel and the Revelation.* Rev. ed. Nashville: Southern Pub. Assn., 1946 (first pub. in 1874).

Spicer, Wm. Ambrose. *Our Day in the Light of Prophecy.* Washington, D. C.: Review and Herald, 1918.

Walker, Allan. *The Law and the Sabbath.* Nashville: Southern Pub. Assn., 1953.

*Yearbook of the Seventh-day Adventist Denomination.* Published annually by the Review and Herald Pub. Co., Washington, D. C. Gives information about world statistics, mission work, educational institutions, hospitals and sanitariums, publishing houses and denominational workers.

GENERAL WORKS:

BOOKS:

Bird, Herbert S. *Theology of Seventh-day Adventism.* Grand Rapids: Eerdmans, 1961. A competent analysis, based on recent sources.

Canright, D. M. *The Lord's Day from Neither Catholics nor Pagans.* New York: Revell, 1915.

————. *Seventh-day Adventism Renounced.* Grand Rapids: Baker, 1961. Originally published in 1889. A former Seventh-day Adventist gives the reasons why he left the denomination, and offers a searching critique of Adventist doctrines.

Douty, Norman F. *Another Look at Seventh-day Adventism.* Grand Rapids: Baker, 1962. A careful, detailed analysis, based on *Questions on Doctrine,* and on a great number of other Seventh-day Adventist publications.

Freiwirth, Paul K. *Why I Left the Seventh-day Adventists.* N.Y.: Vantage Press, 1970. An account of the author's gradual disenchantment with Adventist claims, practices, and doctrines, culminating in his resignation from the church.

Herndon, Booton. *The Seventh Day.* New York: McGraw-Hill, 1960. A very sympathetic treatment. Deals mostly with mission work, but includes brief statements on history, beliefs, and practices.

Martin, Walter R. *The Truth about Seventh-day Adventism.* Grand Rapids: Zondervan, 1960. Defends the view that Seventh-day Adventism is not a cult but a branch of evangelical Christianity. The author is, however, very critical of many Adventist doctrines.

Mitchell, David. *Seventh-day Adventists: Faith in Action.* New York: Vantage Press, 1958. Very sympathetic, though written by a non-Adventist.

Sheldon, Henry C. *Studies in Recent Adventism.* New York: Abingdon, 1915.

Smay, L. J. U. *The Sanctuary and the Sabbath.* Cleveland: Evangelical Association, 1915.

PAMPHLETS:

(Note: These are inexpensive, and may be ordered in quantities for distribution.)

De Korne, J. C. *The Bible and Seventh-day Adventism.* Faith, Prayer, and Tract League; Grand Rapids, Mich. 49504. 15 pp.

Rowell, J. B. *Seventh-day Adventism Examined.* Susanville, Calif.: Challenge Pub. Co., 1952. 52 pp.

Talbot, Louis T. *What's Wrong with Seventh-day Adventism?* Findlay, Ohio: Dunham Pub. Co., 1956. 55 pp.

Tanis, Edward J. *What the Sects Teach.* Grand Rapids: Baker, 1958. 89 pp. A brief critical treatment of Seventh-day Adventism (and of Jehovah's Witnesses, Christian Science, and Spiritism).

(Note: Some of the above pamphlets can be obtained from Religion Analysis Service, 902 Hennepin Ave., Minneapolis 3, Minn.)

PERIODICALS:

Barnhouse, Donald G., and Martin, Walter R. A series of articles on Seventh-day Adventism, which appeared in *Eternity* magazine, Vol. VII, No. 9 — Vol. VIII, No. 1 (Sept., 1956 to Jan., 1957). In these articles the authors first advanced the view that Seventh-day Adventism is not a cult but a branch of evangelical Christianity.

Bear, James E. "The Seventh-day Adventists," *Interpretation,* Vol. X, No. 1 (Jan., 1956), pp. 45-71.

Bird, Herbert S. "Another Look at Adventism," *Christianity Today,* Vol. II, No. 15 (April 28, 1958), pp. 14-17.

Lindsell, Harold. "What of Seventh-day Adventism?" *Christianity Today,* Vol. II. Nos. 13 & 14 (March 31 & April 14, 1958), pp. 6-8, 13-15.

Martin, Walter R. "Seventh-day Adventism," *Christianity Today,* Vol. V, No. 6 (Dec. 19, 1960), pp. 13-15.

Yost, Frank H. "A Seventh-day Adventist Speaks Back," *Christianity Today,* Vol. II, No. 21 (July 21, 1958), pp. 15-18. A reply to Lindsell and Bird.